The

WORLD I IMAGINE

Debbie Jordan

A CREATIVE MANUAL
FOR ENDING POVERTY
AND BUILDING PEACE

Outskirts Press, Inc.
Denver, Colorado

The World I Imagine
A Creative Manual for Ending Poverty and Building Peace
All Rights Reserved.
Copyright © 2008 Debbie Jordan
V2.0

Outskirts Press, Inc.
http://www.outskirtspress.com

ISBN: 978-1-4327-1861-9

Library of Congress Control Number: 2008922635

Outskirts Press and the "OP" logo are trademarks belonging to Outskirts Press, Inc.

PRINTED IN THE UNITED STATES OF AMERICA

Dedication

To Jim, for forty years, for better, for worse, and all the rest.
To Deborah Harris and Sharon Lynn, who helped me remember my goals.
To Frank McGee, whose conversations helped me bring focus to many ideas presented herein.
To Dr. Kenneth D. Paige of Sun Lakes Family Physicians, Sun Lakes, AZ, whose enthusiasm sparked my resolve to turn these essays into a book.
And to all those people who are laboring to end poverty and build a peaceful society--without resorting to violence, which is so obviously counterproductive!

Acknowledgments

This book presents ideas that I've collected over a lifetime from more sources than I can even remember. The process of setting them down and organizing them for publication took a lot of spurs from many people who care, about my work and about my dreams. A few of them must be mentioned here:

Any conversation with the Most Reverend Bennett D.D. Burke, Bishop, Liberal Catholic Diocese of Arizona, helps me focus on the ideas I discuss here.

Even a single idea helps clarify a complicated issue, as happened in one conversation with George and Regina Flores. Thanks, George.

Since 2000, Kayne Crison, editor of *Arizona City Independent Edition*, has held wide open that door through which I've plunged toward my literary dreams.

During my first trip through this publishing maze, Cornelia Nemeth skillfully led the way and provided all the encouragement I needed.

And when I was too young to be taken seriously by the big wide world, a handful of teachers encouraged me to use my imagination, though that detail wasn't in the curriculum.

Ode to War
(Or: Peace is Dull)
by Debbie Jordan (1989)

Peace is dull.
War is far more exciting.
So what if war kills people?

Peace takes a lot of hard work.
Day in and day out,
nothing but sameness;
slow, dull peace.

War may be expensive,
but peace certainly isn't profitable,
except for those privileged few
who rake in
all the profits of war.

Where are the memorials to peace
and the peacemakers?

Table of Contents

Chapter 1

Building Peace without Poverty

THE WORLD I IMAGINE

"**I**f I ruled the earth . . . "

So go the lyrics of an old standard sung by Perry Como ("If," written by Stanley J. Damerell, Torchard Evans, and Robert Hargreaves) way back . . . Well, that's not really important. The point is, the dream of owning supreme power over the planet is not unique.

When I searched online for the lyrics of that song, I discovered that the concept has been repeated over and over, from children's songs ("If Kids Ruled the World," written by Monty Harper for actual children) to rap ("If I Ruled the World Imagine That," penned by Nasir Jones, David Franklin Reeves, Lawrence Smith, and Kurt Walker).

What all these songs have in common are mostly dreams of personal reward, from romance (Como) to "cool cars" and no homework or school (Harper, for the kids) to "smokin weed . . . without cops harassin" (Jones, Reeves, Smith, and Walker). The kids do dream that "No one would be poor," "there'd be no war," and "Everybody will be free"; and the rapster wants to "make Coretta Scott-King mayor" and "open every cell in Attica." And John Lennon did generously "Imagine": "living life in peace," "no need for greed or hunger," "a brotherhood of man," and "the world will live as one."

Halcyon concepts indeed. But while we dream of these goals, we need to understand that peace is not merely the absence of conflict. None of these artists mention the vast amount of labor that will be needed to end poverty and establish a just society for everyone in the world. Such information is too complicated to be contained in a single song. Establishing and maintaining a peaceful world will take a heck of a lot more creativity, dedication, and plain old hard work than the tradition of war ever exacted from the human race. Granted, a true state of peace would be a whole lot cheaper and far less traumatic than any old-fashioned war, but, to date, no one seems to know how to pull it off.

On the other hand, if I ruled the world . . .

I would not rule. I would teach. And I would work to establish a system in which every person receives all the basic goods and services they need to enjoy a dignified existence. Payment for this basic benefit would equal no more than half the full-time wage of the lowest-paid full-time worker on the planet.

This plan can't be explained in a convenient "sound bite," nor can I delineate the concept fully in just a few pages. For every point I present, I can raise at least two more issues that will need explaining, and I'm sure other people will come up with a lot more questions about it than I ever can. But the preceding paragraph, as confusing as it may seem at first, does serve a purpose: It provides a guidepost which can be used to draw a map, charting a route from where our society is now, all the way into a future where no one is forced to exist in a state of poverty and neglect.

But I must be clear about certain points. I'm not talking about classless socialism or a totalitarian government. Those things have been tried and have failed miserably. But then, so has the current system of runaway capitalism that denigrates social conscience. As long as even one person goes hungry, cannot find a job, or is denied protection from abuse, the government we should all be able to depend upon is not working.

But it can work. Every one of these problems could be managed and more, but not the way we're dealing with them now. The current system has too much wasteful redundancy, and too, too many gigantic cracks through which the weakest drop into oblivion. While some people have more than they could ever use, others are denied the help they need to lead productive lives as contributing members of society.

So, while we must be clear about the ends, we must also be diligent about cleaning up the means. We must ensure that no one is being hurt or left behind, and we must ensure that everyone receives the basic services due to every member of a truly just and democratic society.

While I can't remember a time when I didn't believe in this dream, in 1991 I began to fully envision how these principles might work together as we build a society with no poverty or war on our planet. I plan to dramatize the concept in a future novel that will be a companion to this book one day, to demonstrate how my ideas might be implemented in a fully functioning society. Naturally, it will be a fantasy!

Meanwhile, the essays in this book should help to explain the basic principles of this plan and how they can work together. My dream is that we will eventually develop a society in which everyone contributes what they can give and takes away what they need. Beyond that, all those who have the means to do so should be able to purchase any extra goods and services that they can afford.

A dream? Probably. But progress never begins without a germ of an idea from which to grow. Perhaps one day one of the ideas I discuss here will help lead the way to a society that really works.

We can only imagine!

NEEDS VERSUS WANTS

You might remember that commercial for one of those ubiquitous SUVs where the voice-over rattled on about the room, the comfort, and, especially, the power. Finally came the closing message: "It's not more than you need, just more than you're used to."

For the life of me, I cannot figure out how anyone would *need* a gas-guzzling, road-hogging machine so desperately that they could not go on living without one!

That's the real meaning of the word "need." According to the *Oxford American Dictionary* (Pocket Edition, 1980), "need" is defined as: 1. circumstances in which a thing or course of action is required; 2. a situation of great difficulty or misfortune; 3. lack of necessaries, poverty; 4. a requirement, a thing necessary for life.

An SUV doesn't even come close to meeting any of those definitions, except for the most stubbornly selfish among us. For millennia, people have survived just fine without those huge honking machines. On the contrary, that species of hardware is actually contributing to the destruction of our own. Species, that is. You know, global warming and all that. But this awful bit of advertising does help me demonstrate the difference between needs and wants.

The needs I'm referring to are those basic goods and services that every person must have in order to enjoy a dignified existence. The wants are everything else.

For instance, shelter from the elements is a need; a multimillion-dollar mansion is a want. I sure do want that big house, but I can live well enough without it!

Nutritious food is a need; *filet mignon* is a want. The steak might even come from a "mad" cow, so I'm happy with the veggies!

Basic transportation is a need; the aforementioned SUV is just overkill. Besides, we shorties need a ladder just to climb into those hulking machines!

There aren't a whole lot of truly basic human needs, but without any item on the list, a person is denied the right to live in freedom, with dignity. So, to explain my dream of a world in which every person on the planet is guaranteed that right, I've made a list of the basic goods and services that I believe are necessary for a dignified existence.

Besides basic housing, food, and transportation, the list includes but is not limited to: basic clothing, medical and psychological care, dental and vision services, education and job training, child care, public information services such as library and internet access, personal grooming products and basic household furnishings, household cleaning products and repair tools and/or services, public services such as roads and police and fire protection, and even basic funeral and burial services.

Understanding what is basic and what is not is more complicated than this simple list, as I will discuss throughout this book. If every person on the planet actually had everything they need to survive, learn, work, and contribute to society in exchange for these goods and services--and they had no reason to fear losing that right, even for a short period of time--then human beings whose existence is now circumscribed only by fear and conflict would have no reason to challenge any of those people who enjoy so much more than they need in their daily lives.

Then, and only then, will poverty be no more. Only then will humans finally be able to live in true peace on the earth!

Chapter *2*

Meeting Human Needs

DELIVERING SERVICES

I n recent years, the world has witnessed the capitulation of three dictatorships, in Afghanistan, Iraq, and Haiti. Few people would claim that the deposed rulers always provided even the simplest services necessary for the comfort of large sections of their citizenry. Instead, agents of these former governments used violence and terror to exact punishment and extract unquestioning loyalty to Mullah Mohammed Omar and the Taliban, Saddam Hussein, and Jean-Bertrand Aristide.

Sadly, the removal of these ruthless rulers left power vacuums which more strongmen are using to try to establish their own despotic regimes. Under the circumstances, that's almost inevitable. Yet an organization that would deliver the basic necessities to every citizen in these countries, in exchange for each person's corresponding contributions in money and labor to the

7

system, would prevent the development of any new dictatorships and pave the way to the first true democracies on the planet.

This assessment is supported by the lessons of these failed totalitarian governments. The simplest way that a dictator can control a group of people is by controlling everyone's access to the necessities of life. Conversely, the only way to ensure that people are truly free is to expedite the delivery of basic goods and services to every person in the country at a reasonable cost.

No country of any consequence has ever done this successfully. Even the United States, considered the greatest democracy in history, falls woefully short. After more than 200 years, the "great experiment" still fails to provide adequate services to millions of people who are left homeless, hungry, or at least have limited or no access to health care and other necessities of life. Even worse, a shocking number of the poorest people in the country are children!

The reason this problem continues is that all governments, even our own, are ruled from the top down. Decisions affecting human lives are made by politicians and bureaucrats who remain unaffected by the consequences of their judgments. Worse, instead of implementing strategies to provide every citizen with the necessities of life at reasonable cost, policymakers tolerate the perpetuation of the poverty class and make few attempts to improve the status quo.

Though there are scattered efforts to help people at the lowest levels of society, these enterprises have two inherent flaws: The lack of a single comprehensive program to address all the basic needs of all citizens leaves massive gaps in services, especially among the poorest people; and many services are redundant or give help to people who don't need it. The only way to eliminate the costly twin problems of neglect and waste is to implement a unified system that addresses all of our social needs at once.

The solution is simple: Empower people to work in every neighborhood to ensure that each member of the surrounding community receives all the goods and services necessary for a dignified existence. One of the most vital of these services will be to direct unemployed people toward employers who need workers, so every employable person will be able to earn money to pay for everything they need.

Where would these neighborhood service workers come from? Many would be reassigned from their current positions in top-heavy, wasteful--and often ineffectual--social-service agencies to neighborhood centers located in every community, preferably in or near their own neighborhoods. Another source of highly skilled labor for this task would be the numerous private charities currently performing similar work in scatter-shot manner, with mixed results. They would be joined by local people who would assist them in the task of ensuring that everyone in their assigned area receives the minimum benefits they need to enjoy a dignified existence.

Since there would no longer be a need for government or charitable agencies that currently provide a patchwork of services--including welfare, food stamps, employment aid, social security, etc.--the revenue that was previously funneled through those massive bureaucracies would be redirected to pay for those services that are delivered directly to each citizen through the neighborhood centers.

The key to the success of this plan would be to compile a comprehensive list of goods and services that each citizen should receive, as needed. Most importantly, access to basic services must not be controlled by politicians or bureaucrats who now exercise their authority by limiting or denying basic services to certain individuals or groups. With this plan, every single person, without exception, would receive exactly what they need, no more and no less.

If there will be no peace until poverty is eliminated, then only when universal basic support systems--with neither gaps nor redundancies and absolute protection from political manipulation--are implemented will everyone live without fear from individuals and, especially, hostile government forces.

That is the only way to establish complete freedom and a true democracy. It is the only way that people on this earth will finally be able to live together in peace.

DELIVERING GOODS

So far in this book, I've detailed my dream of a global system that would provide every person, at a cost they can afford, with every basic service they need in order to live with dignity. If that were actually to happen, humans would accomplish something that's never been done before: abolish all poverty completely from this earth.

The greatest challenge to this plan would be the logistics of delivering the necessary basic goods to people in every city and town, village and farm, in every corner of the world. On the other hand, certain factors inherent in such a universal system would mean that this plan could be implemented with much less trouble than retailers must deal with now.

The first factor is money. Under the existing system, businesses that sell food, clothing, and shelter, among other things, depend upon consumers being able to pay for these commodities. For example, stores in poor neighborhoods aren't as profitable as those that serve people with higher incomes. With losses from stock they can't sell, bad credit accounts, and theft--much of which is a direct result of poverty--retailers in poor areas often charge more than they would for the same items in stores that serve customers with a lot more money to spend. These inflated prices act as an unfair surcharge imposed upon poor people simply because they are poor. The practice is also one of the many reasons that poor people find it so hard to save enough money to rise above this state of deprivation.

With such economic disparities within industrialized nations, it's easy to see why trying to sell goods in third-world countries--where poverty is far more rampant--is an extremely risky undertaking. But if society would guarantee that every person is able to earn at least twice as much money as it takes for them to pay for all the basic goods and services they need, then most of that risk would disappear. The fact that everyone could pay for all of the basic goods they need would mean that even major retailers could maintain small branch or satellite stores with little or no risk in or near villages and farms in far-flung corners of the world.

The second factor is the availability of trained employees. One problem with our educational system is a lack of adequate job training before young people are sent off into the world of adult employment. That task is usually left to companies that hire people after they've left school. The danger of any company investing money in training is that the employees could then bolt to other companies, taking the benefits of their training with them.

In the later chapter on Universal Education, I detail some ideas to improve this gap in education. For now, I'll say that procedures for training people for various jobs should be established as a joint venture between the community and businesses that hire local residents once they reach a certain level of expertise in their field.

A third factor in the success of any economic venture is the opportunity for growth. Since the absence of a poverty class would assure a strong and consistent basic retail market, the size of the general market would depend even more on the quality and growth of overall employment. Guaranteeing full employment is another facet of my plan, which I discuss in detail in the chapter on Universal Employment.

If everyone had equal access to the basic goods they need for a dignified existence, then many of the social problems we now face would diminish or disappear altogether. If no one worried where their next meal was coming from, where they could find shelter every single night of their lives, or whether serious illness would doom them to a life without hope, then politicians could no longer promise pie-in-the-sky even as they deliver more of the same policies that benefit the few while ignoring the needs of the many.

If there were no more poverty on the planet, then there would be no more excuse for people to resort to violence to obtain the basic goods they need for survival. Only then could we actually begin the task of building a truly peaceful society on the earth.

Chapter *3*

Paying for Human Needs

BASIC TAX PAYMENTS

I n the previous chapter on Meeting Human Needs, I explained how I imagine all the basic goods and services that people need in order to live with dignity could be delivered to everyone in every community around the world. The question is: Who would pay for such a grandiose plan to eliminate poverty from the planet?

In my plan, the cost for all basic personal goods and services would be collected as a basic tax, with the amount imposed on each person depending on where they fall on a scale that accounts for such factors as age and general health, as detailed in the section on age and disability in the chapter on Universal Employment. This basic tax would be no more than half the amount earned by the lowest-paid full-time worker on the planet. While every healthy adult between the ages of 20 and 60 would pay the full amount of this basic tax, people who are younger or older or have a disability that limits their capacity for productive labor would pay discounted tax amounts. With this formula, the youngest and oldest, and those with the most severe disabilities that prevent them from doing any productive work would pay nothing at all.

If this plan were implemented, then even the most menial laborer on the planet would earn at least twice what every other healthy adult--from workers at the bottom level all the way up to the wealthiest corporate executive--pays into the basic fund. In return for this basic tax, everyone would receive all the basic personal supplies and services they need for a dignified existence. In addition, a person could purchase an upgraded or extra product or service by paying the basic cost plus any required general funds to cover the balance of the cost of the product or service. That's why it's vital to identify exactly what constitutes a necessity and what is a mere "want," something the person doesn't actually require to live with dignity and be a productive member of society.

The tool that people would use to track their basic tax payments and purchases would be personal electronic cards similar to the debit cards that banks use today. Because of the importance of the data they carry, these cards would be protected by the most up-to-date identification process, such as eye or hand prints, or both.

Just as my idea to base trained workers and satellite stores in every community worldwide would ensure that every person receives what they need, so my plan for the dispersal of basic tax monies would be more efficient than the expensive piecemeal systems that governments use now. Currently, most taxes are paid directly to a central government, then smaller amounts are dispersed to states, counties, communities, and individual neighborhoods. By the time money reaches the bottom again, where the people who paid the taxes actually live, so many administrative levels have skimmed their share off the top that there's never enough to pay for everything the people actually need.

In my plan, basic taxes would be paid directly to communities, and the money would be used to pay for the basic services and goods everyone receives. Every three months, any excess monies in a community's basic fund would be transferred directly to a collective or universal fund. During the next quarter, proceeds from that fund could be used to supplement any extra basic expenses in communities that require a larger amount than their residents can pay.

For instance, if a particular community spends only 75% of its basic tax monies during the first three months of the year, the remaining 25% of their basic tax monies would be deposited into the universal fund. During the second quarter of the year, communities in another part of the world could draw from the universal fund to help pay for repairing and replacing the basic goods they might have lost during an unusual natural catastrophe, such as a hurricane or an earthquake.

Once these rebuilt communities have a surplus in their basic coffers again, their contributions to the universal fund could help pay to rebuild the first community when it is devastated by a tornado. In addition, communities could draw money from the universal fund on a regular basis to operate central facilities that deliver basic services to people from many communities, such as large medical centers or universities.

The primary reason this system would work is the lack of multiple layers of bureaucracy that are not only expensive but, inevitably, end up cutting some people out of their benefit loop. In the system I imagine, no one would ever be cut from the loop.

So far, I've discussed my plan to pay for the basic personal goods and services everyone needs to receive directly so they would be able to enjoy a dignified existence. In the following section on general tax payments, I explain my plan to pay for the general services that governments provide, such as police and fire protection, roads and highways, and much, much more.

It's easy to imagine how different our lives would be if we could establish a system that seamlessly provides all these services to everyone for a reasonable cost. Indeed, it would take such a systemic and systematic approach to solve the problems we face today and establish true democracy and lasting peace throughout the entire planet.

GENERAL TAX PAYMENTS

So far, I've discussed the ways in which basic personal goods and services could be delivered to everyone on the planet in exchange for their payment of a basic tax that would amount to no more than half of what the lowest-paid full-time worker earns. If this system were implemented, no one would struggle for mere survival and even the most menial laborers could also be able to enjoy some of the good things in life.

But a smoothly functioning society requires more than just a well-oiled retail machine. It takes efficient transportation systems, dependable emergency and utility services, strong security forces, balanced legal services, and many other public-service organizations to support the day-to-day business of the worldwide human community. And all of that takes money!

In my plan, these general services would be paid for

from several sources, not least of which would be a general tax imposed on everything that workers earn above the basic tax levy. A vital difference between my proposal and the current system is that everyone all over the world would be taxed at the same rate, no matter how much money they make.

Three factors would make such an equitable approach possible: With no reason to fear that their basic needs might not be met, workers at the lower end of the pay scale would have no reason to expect wealthy people to carry a larger percentage of the tax burden; full employment would ensure consistent and sufficient tax levies; and without unemployment or poverty, many of the costly institutions we now depend on would be obsolete.

My plan also includes a provision to meet unexpected public costs. While the basic tax levy could be held at the same level year after year, the general tax rate could fluctuate within a preset range, according to the needs of the economy. The principles of equality, with everyone paying the same rate at the same time, and controlled fluctuation, also applied to all equally, could apply to other taxes as well, such as corporate, property, and sales taxes. That consistency and flexibility would ensure that there would always be money for normal expenses, as well as a resource for unusual projects and emergencies.

In fact, when emergencies arise, the ability to tap extra general tax funds on a limited basis would help to shore up the universal fund of basic tax payments that I discussed in the basic tax payments section of this chapter. Moreover, imposing these temporary levies at the same rate worldwide would ensure that there would be plenty of funds to remedy the problem quickly without putting a burden on any group of people or businesses in a particular area.

I also envision one more item being deducted from

everyone's wages, no matter how much or how little money they earn. Five percent of all the money each person earns over their basic tax payment would be deposited into a personally directed investment fund for a minimum of five years, after which time they could liquidate on a tax-free basis any principal that was deposited five years earlier, as well as any earnings on that amount. The money could sit safely in a bank account or a certificate of deposit, or it could be invested in a business or real estate.

This plan would ensure that after five years of employment, everyone would begin to have a steady source of cash they can tap. Even if they spend every penny as it becomes available, at least some funds will be waiting for them until five years after they retire. Of course, it would be ideal if at the end of five years, their experience with the benefits of regular deposits and compound earnings will convince people to keep most or all of the funds invested so they'll have a huge bundle of cash to enjoy in their golden years.

The only restriction I would put on this particular plan is that the funds must be invested only in a licensed institution. No fly-by-night operators need apply, at least where a person's basic payroll investment account is concerned, and these funds could not be invested in such speculative items as art, antiques, or jewelry. Those things are fine for extra investments, but at least part of everyone's assets should be in something solid and relatively predictable.

If everyone invested something in the business engine that runs the economy, it would solidify the system's capacity to maintain full employment. And since everyone would have at least some disposable income, there would be a steady demand for the services and consumer goods that keep companies in business. This source of steady income for those businesses that manufacture quality products or deliver personal services would, in turn, support the system's continuing capacity for full employment. This positive circle of success would guarantee an economy in which no one would have any reason to fear descending into poverty.

Now that I've introduced the basic elements of my dream for a world without poverty, the next chapters in the book address various institutions within the system, such as employment, education, health care, etc. I've tried to be clear enough to answer any questions you might have.

Meanwhile, I hope you've begun to think about the possibility that if everyone earned enough money to pay for all the basic goods and services they need in order to enjoy a dignified existence, poverty would be totally eliminated from the planet. Only then could we finally begin to build a truly peaceful society all over the world.

Chapter 4

Universal Employment

JOBS, WAGES, AND BENEFITS

These days, economic and political fortunes rise and fall on reports of constantly fluctuating employment statistics. As the government releases data on unemployment and jobs created or lost, erratic stock-market prices affect popularity levels of the current administration and, conversely, its competition. The most profound result of all this chaos is the fact that no matter how the government manipulates taxes and interest rates, things just seem to get worse for the most vulnerable members of society, especially the millions of children living in poverty.

But what would happen if everyone had a job that paid at least twice as much as it would take to buy all the basic goods and services needed for a dignified existence? And what if everyone, from CEOs down to the person who sweeps floors for a living, invested at least some money on a regular basis?

Full employment and universal investment are two of

the cornerstones of a smoothly functioning democratic society. The absence of these two conditions is a major reason for the instability of the current system. The challenge is obvious: We must develop a global system in which every person is provided with the means to work, according to their individual skills and abilities, in exchange for an adequate salary.

But where will the jobs come from? I introduced my ideas for a great many jobs, especially in the public sector, in the previous chapter on Meeting Human Needs, and I'll discuss them in more detail in the section on unemployment later in this chapter. For now, let's consider how my plan would affect private-sector employment.

As I explained in the general tax payments section of the chapter on Meeting Human Needs, the combined elements of full employment, adequate pay for all workers, and universal investment would support a stable economic system and benefit well-run businesses. Several other factors in my plan, some of which I mentioned in that earlier chapter, would also help to reach that goal.

Simplifying personal and corporate taxes would ease much of the accounting burden for businesses, and since everyone would receive medical care and other basic services through community programs, employers wouldn't have to deal with insurance matters and optional retirement programs could be simplified. Companies would be free to attract employees with more creative benefits, such as personal services, travel vouchers, etc.

But the issue of salaries is a lot more complicated. To balance flexibility with fairness, industries must establish universal salary ranges for people who perform similar jobs. Variations within these ranges would depend on such factors as an employee's experience, knowledge, and skills, as well as the size of the businesses that employ them.

Companies must also standardize the amount of salaries, bonuses, and stock and options that executives receive.

Ideally, executives' pay and benefits would correspond to what every other employee in the organization receives, and raises and bonuses for everyone at every level of the company would be tied directly to the company's sales performance, which is the only legitimate measure of the success of a business. Incentive pay for creative thinking and exceptional performance on the part of any individual should also be provided, as long as it is given to every employee who earns it, without prejudice.

In addition, communities must standardize the costs for companies to locate facilities in any particular area, and the worldwide community must set and enforce strict guidelines on building codes and pollution controls for everyone, without exception. Implementation of these policies all over the world would eliminate the destructive practice of employers in particular areas undercutting the competition with lower costs at the expense of both workers and the communities in which the businesses are located. Most importantly, it would guarantee a decent standard of living for everyone in the world, as well as a healthy continuation of the single resource that all companies and people depend upon--the planet earth.

Instead of the vicious cycle of poverty and violence that now has us in its grip, society would finally find itself in a positive circle of peace and plenty. Indeed, with no one lacking any of the basics, we can finally live in a society that is truly at peace.

THE FEUDALISM OF LABOR

The Golden Rule of Business, according to a gruesome

pun, is that those who have the gold make the rules. The irony of this old joke is that despite centuries of human development, this sad truth continues to apply in politics, business, and even religion. For instance, no matter how hard people try to improve relations between labor and management, business continues to function according to a model that was the rule during the Middle Ages.

In the feudal model of medieval times, virtually all power over the lives of the working class rested in the hands of the aristocracy. The lord owned all land in the vicinity of the manor house, while serfs lived in humble dwellings on the estate and spent their entire lives toiling for the benefit of the landlord. Everything they needed to support their meager existence was granted to the working poor only at the behest of the nobleman. Any benefit they received was derived from the capricious whims of the lord and master.

Those serfs who made the mistake of displeasing the master were promptly dismissed, not only from their jobs but from the estate itself. They and their families were forced out of their homes, often the only homes they'd ever known, and thrown off the estate. They could no longer receive any of the benefits they'd enjoyed when they were in the good graces of the boss, the landlord.

If all this sounds familiar, then you understand that no matter how many centuries have elapsed, business has not yet evolved beyond this archaic feudal model. In the modern world, not only do bosses hold the power to hire and fire people, but in the United States, they even control the amount and quality of medical services that employees receive and how much it will cost--if they're even allowed to receive those services at all.

And just as it was in the Middle Ages, those who occupy the highest positions of corporate power control their own salaries and benefits, and they hold the power to limit the amount of money and benefits their underlings receive. In fact, the easiest way for corporate executives to increase their own income is to limit the amount of money that other people receive. Worse, executives who lay off thousands of workers usually receive bonuses in the millions of dollars as a reward for performing that odious task.

In the current system, this practice is touted as sound business economics, but it's a disaster for the overall national and world economy and a terrible sociological model as well. The real cost of unemployment is both personal--loss of income, limited or no access to health care, depleted savings, increased debt, foreclosure, bankruptcy--and universal--wasted labor resources and an unproductive drain on the public coffers.

One change from the days when landlords threw vassals off their estates is that companies now give severance pay to some people, which means shelling out money for no work, and states provide a small unemployment stipend, again for no labor in return. The trouble is, unemployment benefits don't cover the cost of food and shelter for the average family, not to mention the other costs of maintaining a decent lifestyle. And many U.S. companies add insult to injury with a cruel joke called COBRA, the post-employment health-insurance plan that costs almost as much as unemployment benefits and doesn't even pay for most real medical expenses.

Just like the harsh landlord-serf relations in feudal times, the modern pattern of employment and unemployment makes no sense. It's time for a big change in the way people are hired and fired and how they are managed as labor resources when they find themselves between permanent private-sector positions.

In the following section on unemployment, I detail a plan that would allow people who are discharged from private-sector jobs to work in their local communities for similar rates of pay until they find new positions with private employers. This would eliminate the negative impact of unemployment on individuals and communities and provide a fluid labor pool for community projects that now go undone.

And replacing employer-provided medical insurance that ends when an employee is terminated with universal single-payer health services would mean not only that everyone would receive medical care when they need it, but the cost of that care would be lower than it is under the current for-profit system.

Obviously, my plan would eliminate the costly financial burden that unemployment puts on workers in the middle and lower classes. What's more, in the world I imagine, people at the top of the corporate ladder would no longer be able to profit by wreaking havoc on the lives of people in the lower ranks. On the contrary, as I explained in the earlier section on jobs, wages, and benefits, the amount of all executive income and benefits would be tied directly to corporate performance--actual sales and delivery of services--as well as the level of income and benefits granted to all the other people who work for the company. So the more effectively workers are able to perform on the job, the more both they and their bosses would benefit, and vice-versa. There should be no other economic model in place.

Perpetuating a negative employment model simply because that's the way it's always been done is just one example of why we need to formulate a completely new approach to all the problems of society. And we must make sure none of the so-called solutions that are tried end up causing problems for anyone, as so many of them do now.

The most important thing we must do is establish a society in which each person is able to purchase all the basic goods and services necessary for a dignified existence at a cost of no more than half the amount earned by the lowest-paid full-time worker on the planet. Only then will we be able to end poverty everywhere.

Only then will humans be able to build a truly peaceful society all around the world.

UNEMPLOYMENT

With so much bad news over the last few years, the reports that have the most profound personal effect on the largest number of people involve the record numbers of job losses, especially in the higher-paying tech sector, and the massive cutbacks in social services. While most people wonder when--or even if--this situation will improve, I prefer to think much farther ahead by imagining the possibility of establishing a system that would actually work for everybody.

It wouldn't be easy. We can't solve the problems that exist in any particular country until the same principles are applied equally to every person all over the world. That means making sure that everyone, no matter where they live or what type of work they perform, has the means to earn at least twice as much as it would cost to purchase all the basic goods and services they need to enjoy a dignified existence.

In the previous section in this chapter on jobs, wages, and benefits, I explained some of my ideas for improving conditions for people working in the private sector. But society must also find a more positive way to manage one of the most personally devastating problems of our economic system: unemployment.

There is no way to avoid the fact that when business slows down, companies have to lay off employees, and they must be allowed to exercise the right to fire those people who don't perform their jobs satisfactorily. But taking steps to cushion the blow for the individuals affected will prevent many of the problems that people, and society as a whole, must now deal with in those circumstances.

Transferring the burden of providing the basic benefit of health care and other benefits from employers to communities, as I explained in the section on jobs, wages, and benefits, will eliminate one of the biggest problems that people now face when they lose their jobs. The other challenge is to ensure that everyone continues to have the means to earn enough money to handle the rest of their financial obligations, so they don't automatically drop down to a lower economic status because of a temporary employment setback. The only way to ease the problem of unemployment would be to establish a system that provides continuous employment for everyone at salary levels similar to those offered in the private sector.

In my plan, as soon as a person receives notice that their current job is ending, they would report to their local community center to receive a temporary assignment to a public-service position. If possible, they would be assigned to a position in their own community, or they should be able to work as close to their home as feasible. They would then spend much of their workday serving in that position until they found another private-sector job--hopefully one that is at least comparable the one they lost.

They would also spend some time during each workday studying an internet database that would detail every job available throughout the world, sending out resumes and making phone calls to potential employers, as well as going out on job interviews. While companies would be free to use private employment agencies, every employer would also be required to post information about all available jobs on this universal database. In time, this democratic tool would trim much of the costs that companies now pay to find suitable candidates for their open positions.

This system would offer a win-win-win solution for everyone involved. Employees would lose neither income nor benefits during the time that they find themselves between private-sector jobs. Businesses wouldn't have to pay for unemployment insurance, and they would also be relieved of the burden of providing severance pay or extended benefits packages upon dismissals, unless they contracted to do so as an added benefit at the time they hired the employee. Companies would also have the flexibility to lay off employees for short periods of time during temporary downturns with little or no financial repercussions to either party, then rehire them when business picks up later. And communities would benefit from a rotating pool of talent offering extra services for their citizens.

There would also be an indirect benefit to this plan. With no reason for people to worry about lost income due to unexpected job loss, consumer spending would be steadier and so would the overall employment picture. That would mean that companies would have no need to resort to the massive layoffs that are so prevalent in the current unpredictable--and unmanageable--economy.

Ideally, some of these temporary public workers might find public service so satisfying that they would decide to continue in that position and stop looking for another job in the private sector. And the flexibility of this system would allow people to switch from permanent to temporary employment and back again as their situations changed, with no change of or gap in the benefits that everyone receives anyway.

One more service that would support the job search would be the public/private job-training program which I mentioned in the chapter on Meeting Human Needs when I discussed my plan for delivering goods. I expand upon this topic in the chapter on Universal Education in the section on learning to work. This service would help employees adapt to changing job markets while they hone their skills for various jobs. It would also provide employers with a large pool of well-trained personnel.

As with every other aspect of my plan, ensuring continuous employment for everyone will make it possible for everyone to earn enough money to purchase all the basic goods and services they need to enjoy a dignified existence, as well as the money they need to take care of their other financial obligations. The resulting personal economic stability would support a consistent consumer base and strengthen the overall economy.

All these factors would provide the building blocks to help eliminate poverty and establish a truly peaceful and democratic society all over the planet.

AGE AND DISABILITY

In the 1960s, a man in Oklahoma faced serious obstacles in his quest to receive an education. His blindness wasn't the problem; it was the state's insistence that he was only qualified to run a concession stand. That official policy toward blind people who needed help to pay for their education explains the stereotype of visually impaired concession-stand operators throughout the United States.

But Ed had a different dream for his life. After earning a degree from the University of Oklahoma, he moved to Texas and worked as a massage therapist before being accepted into chiropractic college. When my husband, Jim, and I were his patients from the late '70s to 1991, he didn't need x-rays, nor did he even have to actually touch our backs to locate the source of our pain. The radiant heat he felt inches from the source told him exactly where we were hurting!

Dr. Ed's struggle to use his gift shows why society must treat people as individuals, not categories. This is even more vital for people with severe health problems and those who are vulnerable because of age. As Pearl S. Buck wrote in "My Several Worlds" (John Day Company, 1954): "Our society must make it right and possible for old people not to fear the young or be deserted by them, for the test of a civilization is the way that it cares for its helpless members."

Throughout this book, I discuss many things that people in the world I imagine should do to help themselves and others enjoy a full and peaceful existence without poverty, but extra care must be made to help people with special needs enjoy full citizenship in a peaceful society. And since each individual has different needs and abilities, the rule for any person with special needs should be that there are no rules, or at least very few of them!

For instance, in the world I imagine, blind people with a gift for healing would receive all the education they need to spend their lives helping others--as Dr. Ed did, despite a discriminatory and archaic government policy. Of course, the same provision should be made for all sighted people who are meant to heal. The only rule that should be engraved in stone would be the one that dictates a practical approach to people with various disabilities and those of various ages so that they can be productive citizens, just like everyone else. Most importantly, all these people should be able to purchase all the basic goods and services they need to enjoy a dignified existence in exchange for their share of contributions to society, which would vary according to an individual's capacity to perform.

In my plan, every healthy person below the age of 20 and over the age of 60 would pay a sliding-scale percentage of the basic tax paid by healthy adults between the ages of 20 and 60, as detailed in the section on basic tax payments in the chapter on Paying for Human Needs. Currently, Americans who retire as early as the age of 62 receive a percentage of their Social Security benefits, which are based on their previous earnings. If they do earn any wages above a certain amount, their Social Security benefits are lowered even more. If they retire later, their benefit percentage goes up, until they reach a certain age, depending on their birth year. Besides being extremely complicated, the system is predicted to collapse in the foreseeable future.

In the world I imagine, healthy adults from 20 to 60 would pay the same basic tax amount in exchange for all the basic goods and services they need. When they turn 61, their basic tax assessment would be lowered by 10% of the full levy each year until they reach the full retirement age of 70. Then for the rest of their lives, they would pay no more basic tax but would receive all the basic goods and services they ever need. These graduated retirement benefits would be the same for every person past the age of 60, no matter how much money they earn. However, they'd continue paying the general tax on all earnings above the basic tax at the same rate as everyone else, as detailed in the general tax payments section of the chapter on Paying for Human Needs.

Beginning at the age of 61, the basic community-service hours that each person would be required to contribute, as detailed in the upcoming community service section of the chapter on Administering a Peaceful Planet, would be reduced by 10% each year until a person turned 65. From that point, all healthy individuals would devote half the amount of basic service hours in their community that healthy people between the ages of 20 and 60 would contribute.

Obviously, this arrangement would make it easier for every healthy citizen to plan how they'll enjoy their "golden" years, since their expenses and benefits would be predictable and stable for the rest of their lives. They would also be able to work as much as they choose without losing any of the benefits they're entitled to receive.

In addition, no one would fear that serious illness or accident would force them to liquidate everything it took them a lifetime of hard work to accumulate just so they can beg for a few crumbs of sub-standard care while they spend the rest of their lives wallowing in poverty.

A similar system of graduated basic payments would be in place for children below the age of 20, along with age-appropriate labor contributions associated with education and job training, as explained in the section on useful learning in the chapter on Universal Education. This system would ensure that children everywhere would receive all the goods and services they need to enjoy a dignified existence, as they grow steadily into the habit of being contributing members of society.

Meanwhile, it is vital to remember that society will only truly honor the rights of every person, no matter their age or physical condition, when the lowest-paid full-time worker on the planet is able to earn at least twice as much as it costs to pay for all the basic goods and services necessary for a dignified existence. Only then will we be able to build a society in which no one is forced to live in a state of need because of age or medical status. Only then will we be able to ensure that every person, no matter their age or physical condition, can enjoy the benefits of living in a truly peaceful world.

Chapter 5

Administering a Peaceful Planet

COMMUNITY SERVICE

A 2004 article profiled four One-Stop Centers in the Phoenix area where job seekers could access the internet, fax machines, and counselors to help them with their job search. Strangely, the supervisor at one center said, "I feel like we are the best-kept secret. A lot of people don't know we are around." (*Arizona Republic*, April 18, 2004, page EC1)

At the time, I wondered why these services weren't available at every Department of Economic Security-- unemployment, among other social services--office throughout the state. I'm happy to report that those services have finally been implemented to a wider degree, so Arizona citizens can now conduct much of their job search from home, via the internet and even over the phone. The large centers are now used for workshops, seminars, and job fairs to help people improve their interviewing skills and meet potential employers.

As I explained in the section on unemployment in the previous chapter on Universal Employment, complete job-search support should be just one of the basic services available in every neighborhood community center throughout the world. That sort of decentralization is key to my plan to eliminate poverty by ensuring that everyone is able to purchase all the basic goods and services they need to enjoy a dignified existence for no more than half what the lowest-paid full-time worker earns.

The backbone of this plan would be the workers assigned to community centers located in every neighborhood. The scope of their duties would be tremendous, but their satisfaction in seeing everyone benefit from their efforts--unlike the current system, which seems designed to deny services to as many people as possible--would support a consistently high level of morale among their ranks.

In previous chapters, I've mentioned three sources for these community employees: people who now labor in public departments and private organizations that would become obsolete under my plan; workers with skills ranging from assembly lines to boardrooms and who find themselves temporarily "at liberty"--between jobs; and people who would dedicate at least a small amount of their time to helping their neighbors, their families, and even themselves.

The basis for the third group would derive from the fact that my plan would require everyone to perform some type of community service for at least a few hours a week. The total amount of time each person would be required to spend in weekly service would depend on their age and physical condition, with healthy adults between the ages of 20 and 60 required to contribute the most time, as well as the needs of the community at any given time.

In the world I imagine, people would be free to manage their community service contributions in many ways. For instance, someone who is traveling can contribute service in a local community wherever they happen to be when they have the time to do it. Or they might combine their total service for an entire month into a single week. This would allow both individuals and communities the flexibility to manage service time as it is available and needed.

While the current system provides no monetary reward for people who volunteer for nonprofit agencies and many interns who toil at for-profit companies, my plan would require that everyone who performs any type of labor, either in their community or at a private company, would be adequately compensated for all of their efforts.

Even the basic community service time that everyone would have to perform would be compensated, so there would be no reason for anyone to resent the requirement. Many people could even pick up extra money now and then by working more hours through their local community center whenever it's convenient for them to do so.

In my plan, for-profit businesses would have to pay everyone who performs any type of work at a rate at least equal to the minimum wage. Companies would no longer be allowed to benefit from unpaid interns, who often work for nothing more than the hope of obtaining a paid position at some indeterminate future date. Neither would the hospitality industry, to name just one example, be allowed to pay less-than-minimum (slave!) wages to people who hope to receive enough money in tips so they can support their families.

The reward that each citizen would receive for performing the minimum amount of community service would be credit toward their basic tax payment, which would combine with their basic tax to pay for all the basic personal goods and services they need. Their duties would depend on their skills balanced with the needs of the community. And unlike the current system, which pays government workers much less than they can receive in the private sector, community service would be compensated according to the same pay ranges detailed in the section on jobs, wages, and benefits in the previous chapter on Universal Employment.

One more source of public labor would be the people who are sentenced to perform community service as punishment for breaking the law. I discuss that subject in more detail in the section on justice and responsibility in the chapter on True Justice.

In the needs versus wants section of the chapter on Building Peace without Poverty, I listed several areas that would be overseen by the workers at community centers. Short-term specialized services might be available at these neighborhood centers, such as emergency medical services or a counselor for people in the midst of a personal crisis. Any major or long-term care in these areas would then be provided by professionals in private practice or at centralized medical centers. In other situations, local community center workers would direct neighborhood residents to all the various public agencies and private companies that offer the entire range of basic goods and services that their circumstances require.

Three more factors make my plan different from the current system: Each community center would be open 24 hours a day, with at least two people on duty at any given time. Every person, no matter their station in life or what they do for a living, must spend a minimum amount of time each month helping someone in need, such as a disabled or an older person, especially by performing some simple service, such as sweeping or mopping a floor or scrubbing a toilet, according to their ability to perform that type of work. And many of the workers at each center would form the basis for a truly democratic form of government that would have no need of political parties. I will detail that remarkable concept in the next section of this chapter on administrating upward.

With basic personal goods and services available for everyone when they need them and a truly democratic system of government, most of the problems we face today would diminish or disappear altogether, especially the condition of poverty. Only when that happens would humans be able to enjoy a world truly at peace.

ADMINISTRATING UPWARD

Like Olympic athletes, Americans become embroiled in competition every four years, but the goals are not mere medals of gold, silver, or bronze. These prizes are the highest offices in the land--actually, the world.

And while judges in athletic contests might risk their reputations by casting a bad vote, for the judges in elections, the stakes are much higher and far more personal. The consequences to voters can mean the difference in their livelihoods, their futures, sometimes even their very lives.

Still, from time immemorial, humans have searched for a few people who could lead them--but to what?

To victory, sometimes. To prosperity. To happiness, or at least the pursuit thereof. We all have dreams of what we expect from our government. The trouble is, most people consider little beyond what they want for themselves and the people closest to them. Few understand that a successful government must guide everyone to victory over poverty, support prosperity for every person on the planet, and establish a society in which no person or group is able to hold sway over or deny the rights of any other person or group.

So what about government by the people? Look around at all the people without jobs, the children who go to bed hungry, entire families left homeless--so many human beings whose needs are ignored--and you can easily see that we aren't even close to building a truly effective, successful society, even in the United States.

But what if everyone had a job that paid at least twice as much as it would cost to purchase all the basic goods and services they need to enjoy a dignified existence? Would we then have a democracy?

Not necessarily. Freedom is more than just doling out benefits. Democracy is not a noun, it is a verb, a state of constant action. True democracy requires committed citizens who respect the basic rights of every human being. A truly democratic government would be run by people dedicated to serving the needs of everyone, not merely a favored few.

The people who currently run governments can be elected or appointed, or they might inherit the office. Some take control by force, but the problem with that scenario should be painfully obvious. Many start at the bottom and work their way up, but government experience isn't required to jump into the arena at any level, even for the top job. On the contrary, money and connections are often more useful for winning public office than a lifetime spent working for the good of the people that the government should be serving.

On the other hand, in the world I imagine, all government employees, from the bottom all the way to the top of the pyramid, would begin by serving the people in their own communities. They would be the ones who are willing to help their neighbors, not merely in emergencies but with everyday problems, and who help develop, implement, and share the ideas that make society work for everyone.

My plan would require that anyone who hopes to fill the top job could only get there by serving at least one term at each level of government, starting with local service in or close to their own neighborhood, before moving up to the next level, and so on up the ladder. And no one would fill a slot on their own but would serve as part of a committee of people with similar responsibilities, all the way up to the top job--or jobs--in the world. In addition, one person would lead a committee for no more than a year at a time. Then the chair would rotate to another person on that committee for the next year. During the year that a member occupied the chair, they would not be able to vote on any decision except when it's necessary to break a tie.

Committee members would also be subject to term limits, but not the current policy of "two terms and you'll never darken that office again." That wastes not only talent but years of experience. In my plan, the term of any office would be two years in duration, no matter the level of service, and no one would serve at any single level for more than two consecutive terms. Then they must either be elected to the next level up or serve at least one term at a level below that committee level, depending on the amount of time they stay away from public service, before they can serve at that level again. That means if they leave public service for any length of time, getting back into the pyramid of service could mean starting again as low as the community level, unless they spend time serving on a sub-committee, as detailed in the next section on committee support.

Using the current government model as an example, consider the course that a person could take after finishing two terms as mayor of a city. Actually, under my plan, they would have been one of several co-mayors with two of them having served in the chair position in one of the two years of their concurrent terms. With my plan, they would either move up to a position in the state legislature or serve another term on the city council or at a local community center before they can join the mayoral committee again.

Another difference I imagine would be that instead of aligning themselves with opposing political parties, people serving in government positions would represent various groups from the general population, based on age, gender, ethnicity, health status, and various other differences that now divide people instead of uniting them.

Of course, one member would naturally match more than one factor and, thus, stand for several groups at the same time. For example, a single Latino in his 20s who uses a wheelchair would represent at least three groups, while a white woman in her 40s with children and grandchildren, who controls her diabetes with diet and exercise, would reflect and represent many different types of people from those the young man typifies.

In upcoming sections on practicing democracy in the chapter on Establishing True Democracy and the section on making just laws in the chapter on True Justice, I discuss the responsibilities of certain committees I envision in more detail. For now, I hope people will think about a system in which everyone in government service would truly represent every member of society instead of the entities that constitute the real "special interests," such as oil companies, utilities, and the for-profit medical industry.

If such a committee system were to take the place of the limited party government we have now, we would be able to take a giant step toward eliminating poverty and establishing a truly democratic and peaceful society throughout the world, for the first time in history.

COMMITTEE SUPPORT

In the section in this chapter on administrating upward, I discussed the concept of having committees, rather than individuals, to serve in various government offices. Besides the obvious benefit of diluting the potentially dangerous influence of personal power, it would mean that the duties of office would be shared by several people at once. It would also mean that the committee could handle more responsibilities and accomplish more than is possible with the single-person model now in use.

But even committee members would need support staff, and they would need to know that someone was trained to take over a seat on the committee if something ever happened to one or more of the members. In the world I imagine, both roles would be filled by a group of people who would serve on sub-committees.

In my plan, each sub-committee would consist of at least two people whose job would be to support the work of each member of a committee, so each sub-committee would consist of at least twice as many members as the committee it serves. The primary task of sub-committee members would be to supervise any other staff members who would help elected committee members fulfill their duties.

Like committee members, sub-committee members would have to work their way up the ladder step-by-step, and they would have to reflect the diversities of the general population in gender, age, ethnicity, health status, etc.

Unlike committee members who are elected, sub-committee members would be appointed by the committee members they'd work for, and their duties would be similar to those of senior aides who now serve politicians.

Sub-committee members would oversee such details as scheduling, speech writing, phone calls, correspondence, and the myriad other minutiae of their committee member's responsibilities. In addition, at least one of each committee member's sub-committee aides would be present at each committee meeting, and each sub-committee member would be required to attend at least half the regular meetings held by committee members.

Obviously, the intimate knowledge that sub-committee members would have with a committee member's duties would give them the skills they'd need to step sideways into a committee seat, or at least into a committee at any level below the highest one they'd served as a sub-committee member. In my plan, skilled sub-committee members wouldn't have to go back to the community level to move into the committee system. Besides being able to run for a committee seat up to the level they'd served as sub-committee member, they would also be a valuable resource in case of an unexpected opening on a committee.

Sub-committee members would supervise professionals, such as researchers, speech writers, computer technicians, etc., along with junior staff members, including full- and part-time workers. While none of these support people could move directly onto a committee as sub-committee members could, these staff jobs would give them experience with day-to-day government operations in case they wanted to return to their communities to begin serving on committees or as sub-committee aides, and eventually move up the ladder as their former bosses had done.

Since sub-committee members wouldn't be elected, there would be no restrictions on the length of time they could spend serving at any sub-committee level or working for a particular committee member. On the other hand, voluntary mobility among sub-committee members would avoid an undue concentration of power. Even better, the more levels of operation that a person is able to experience at different levels of administration, the more valuable they would be to the system and the greater their understanding of the "big picture" of the relationship between government and society.

Their familiarity with government operations should especially help sub-committee members grasp the importance of the ultimate goal of ensuring that the lowest-paid full-time worker on the planet earns at least twice as much as it would take to purchase all the basic goods and services needed to enjoy a dignified existence.

Under my plan, one of the most important duties of sub-committee members would be to expedite communications between committee members and the citizens they would serve. In the section on practicing democracy in the chapter on Establishing True Democracy, I'll discuss more about that relationship and, especially, how it would enable the establishment and practice of real democracy of the sort that has yet to be practiced on this planet.

Only when we completely eliminate poverty from the planet and build a true democracy that serves the needs of every citizen will we be able to build a truly peaceful society around the world.

Chapter **6**

Political Campaigns and Elections

DEMOCRATIC ELECTIONS

A s if the election controversy of 2000 weren't bad enough, a 2004 AP article revealed the disturbing fact that less than 25% of the adult population actually voted for the president. That's because most eligible voters don't even bother to cast a ballot, and the winner often receives less than half of the votes cast!

Add the fact that almost a billion dollars was spent for the top job in 2004, and it's obvious we need a radical change in the electoral process before this country's ship of state can be set on an even keel!

The problem, according to experts, is due to the general dissatisfaction that most people have with the political system in this country. Americans don't believe that the country that touts itself as the most democratic in the world is even a democracy at all. It's obvious we need to make serious changes in order to fundamentally alter the power structure that now controls our government and, thus, our lives.

In the administrating upward section of the previous chapter on Administering a Peaceful Planet, I introduced several ideas that would change the nature of political office. The goal is to remove the potential for power that politicians too often abuse, while ensuring that they actually fulfill the roles they were hired to perform in the first place.

But reform will never be possible until we also simplify the way candidates are chosen. My suggestions that each office consist of a committee, instead of a single person, and that candidates reflect various groups in the population they will serve, based on gender, age, ethnicity, health status, etc., would diminish the power of political parties, if not eliminate them altogether.

Just imagine, if there were no more Republicans or Democrats. Then our government would no longer be divided between powerful business and other special interests competing with all the people who are primarily fighting for their basic rights to good paying jobs, reasonably priced goods and services, and clean water and fresh air.

In the community service section of the previous chapter on Administering a Peaceful Planet, I detailed some ways in which everyone would spend time serving their community. This aspect of my plan to build a cohesive society would encourage greater participation in the political process by giving voters deeper insight into the professional and personal qualifications of the people that they elect to public office, especially at or near the local level.

Moreover, my plan for term limits--that no one serve in any single position for more than two consecutive terms--while not as strict as current term limits, would at least prevent anyone from becoming an entrenched power player at any level of service. And my suggestion that terms for any office be limited to two years means that within four years, at most, everyone would have to move to a different level--or even out--of the public-service sector. They could return to the previous position only after they've served in another capacity for a while.

Of course, two or more people could alternate terms in a particular position, with each providing their unique talents to the job at different times. The trouble is, they could also cooperate in an old-fashioned power play. That's why it would be necessary to design other factors into the system to limit the amount of power that any person or group of people could exercise in the capacity of public service.

In the following sections of this chapter, I will detail my ideas for limiting campaign costs, providing all candidates with equal access to free media services, and reforming the electoral process in order to prevent the sort of vote-counting fiascos that occurred in the most recent presidential elections.

Yet, even as we consider reforming some of the minute details of government, we must always remember that the ultimate goal is to simplify the currently unworkable system in order to build a society in which everyone is able to earn at least twice as much money as it would take to purchase all the basic goods and services they need to enjoy a dignified existence. Only then will we be able to eliminate poverty and establish a truly peaceful society around the world.

"PAYING" POLITICS

Which came first, big campaign spending or big campaign donations? Politicians seem to expand campaign spending to use all the money they receive, no matter where it comes from; and many campaigns are run on credit, leaving large debts after the election, win or lose. Yet any attempt to limit political donations won't work until drastic changes are made in the way campaigns are conducted.

Despite recent laws designed to curb campaign spending, almost a billion dollars was spent on the top job during the 2004 election. That's why I've decided once more to put in my two cents--a sort of campaign spending limit, as it were.

Obviously, some limits must be set on money spent on bumper stickers, pins, hats, balloons, and the outrageous costs of travel, hotels, restaurants, etc. But changing the ways in which candidates and political parties advertise would go a long way toward stemming the excessive flow of cash currently being wasted on the electoral process. And though nothing will prevent some people from choosing candidates for emotional reasons, especially when their choices are based on single issues, changing the nature of media advertising would provide intelligent voters with more information on issues and candidates than they now receive, and for a lot less money.

The only way to reduce spending is to limit the most expensive item in campaign budgets: media advertising. This could be done by restricting canned political ads to a single system that could be called Political Access Networks (PAN). A publicly supported and run access channel could be transmitted to every person in the country who has a radio or TV set, via cable, satellite, and local broadcasting systems. To complete the media package, PAN could also publish a political newspaper with the same purpose as the TV and radio networks. And since the internet has become such a vital part of campaigning lately, PAN could maintain a web site where anyone could find detailed information on every candidate in any race in the country, including links to each candidate's campaign web site.

Part of the cost of running the PAN system could come from a surtax on candidate filing fees, along with other public and private sources. Some tax money from the general tax fund, which I detailed in the chapter on Paying for Human Needs, could be used to support the PAN networks. Fees could be charged to all political parties, as long as they continue to be part of the electoral process, as well as other media organizations which would also work in concert with PAN to broadcast political news. Monies for the PAN system could be pooled nationally and distributed directly to all local PAN studios and distributors as needed to make sure every candidate has complete and equal media access.

With free media access through PAN, candidates would no longer buy ad time on other radio or TV stations, but all candidates, regardless of party affiliation, would be given equal access to non-PAN media via personal appearances on news, talk, and magazine programs.

As with the PAN TV and radio networks, PAN News would offer free ad space to all candidates during campaigns, as well as news stories on candidates and issues. Between campaigns, the PAN Networks and News will update citizens on political issues and potential candidates.

While PAN's web site and TV and radio stations would be available 24 hours a day, the PAN newspaper could be distributed up to twice a week during campaigns, and at other times it could be published monthly or semi-monthly. Copies would be distributed to every household, via mail or neighborhood carriers, and it could be available in racks outside retail outlets, such as grocery, drug, discount, and department stores.

One great benefit of PAN would be the fact that ads for all candidates for each office can be accessed in the same place. With ads for all candidates for any single office running in succession, voters would have a better chance to compare all candidates for each office as objectively as possible. In the next section of this chapter on running a clean campaign, I'll share more details about how PAN would help citizens make better decisions in the voting booth.

I first introduced this concept for campaign reform in the *Arizona City Independent Edition* in 1991, and nothing has improved in all that time. In fact, the situation has deteriorated and is worse than ever. Obviously, I'm going to keep on talking up the subject every chance I get. Maybe one day it'll do some good. You never can tell!

A CLEAN CAMPAIGN

Ideally, political campaigns would be a contest between the brightest public servants, people who've dedicated their lives to making society work for everyone. Instead, some politicians live and die by the amount of money they raise and consider new ideas to be not only personal attacks, but acts of treason. They drag campaigns down to the level of street fights, and for months before an election, they pollute the airwaves with venom 24 hours a day.

I'm sure many people share my desire for more positive

debate on all the issues. That's why I'd like to see ads for every candidate aired by a national media service like the one I detailed in the previous section of this chapter on "paying" politics.

The first rule of Political Access Networks (PAN) would be to provide each candidate for any office with free TV and radio time, along with free print space in the companion PAN newspaper and free space and a link to their own campaign web site on the PAN web site. PAN would provide equipment at no charge so candidates can produce their own video spots, though wealthier candidates could be free to provide more professional videos of their own. Cost limits would be established though, and candidates could offer no more than one new ad within a prescribed period, such as once a week.

Each candidate's ad would be required to last from five to ten minutes. The minimum length would necessitate weightier content than the usual "family-dog-flag-apple pie" symbols--which should be discouraged in favor of more intellectual content--while the upper limit would ensure that each candidate's message would be heard and several of these spots could be run during each hour of air time.

During campaigns, each six-hour block of programs would be repeated to fill the 24-hour day. It would be divided between ads for national, regional, and local candidates and political news and discussion programs. Between campaigns, potential candidates could keep their names before the public by participating in an expanded roster of these news and discussion programs.

All PAN programming would focus on political issues. It would be professionally produced and, where appropriate, edited to hold the interest of people who want high quality political programming. Costs could be contained by limiting PAN-produced material to the simple "talking heads" format. Tapes of these discussion programs could be made available to other media, as well as schools and libraries. Tape sales to commercial outlets could also provide extra revenue to defray the cost of running the PAN networks.

Each candidate would be required to engage in at least one debate with every candidate running for the same office, except by mutual agreement. Thus, no candidate who wants to participate can be blocked from a debate, as major parties often do to third-party candidates. For instance, Bill Smith, Bob Jones, and Sally Williams are running for the same office. Smith, an independent, chooses to debate the others, so Jones and Williams must debate him. By mutual agreement, Jones and Williams, the major party candidates, forgo their joint debate, so Smith faces each one separately.

Other news organizations would provide PAN with tapes of all appearances, interviews, and debates with all candidates after they run on their own networks. For instance, after PBS or CNN host a debate between presidential candidates, PAN would rerun the debate a minimum of 16 times: repeated four times on each of at least four nonconsecutive days. Interviews that might run once on a network magazine show would be rerun many times on PAN, giving voters greater opportunity to study candidates before going to the polls.

Candidates would be restricted in the type of campaign literature they could produce, thus saving a great deal of money now wasted in political campaigns. For instance, because the PAN Newspaper would provide free ad space and be universally distributed, candidates could engage in limited mass mailings, and they would be restrained from engaging in the sort of "dirty tricks" mailings that some politicians and parties use now, often just before an election.

By focusing political discussions through a controlled forum like PAN, as well as implementing changes in political offices, as detailed in the administrating upward section of the chapter on Administering a Peaceful Planet, the open warfare that some politicians engage in these days would diminish, or even disappear. Even better, these changes would mitigate the power that the almighty dollar-- actually those who control more of it--has held over the ballot box in recent years.

If governments were to establish positive political systems, for the first time in history, it would finally be possible for people to begin working toward building a society in which every person could earn at least twice as much money as it would take to purchase all the basic goods and services they need to enjoy a dignified existence. And with no more conflict in the political arena, we could begin to focus our resources toward eliminating war from the entire planet, for the first time in history.

MAKING VOTES COUNT

The best thing that can be said about American politics in the last couple of months of 2000 is that it provided a perfect example of how not to run an election!

So far in this book I've tried to focus more on solutions than the problems they might help to resolve. On this subject, however, I come dangerously close to blowing my- -admittedly uncustomary--ladylike demeanor. Though I try to avoid outright partisanship in this discussion, I must emphasize that this country must take steps to establish a truly democratic electoral system so that no other person will ever be able to claim the office of president despite receiving fewer votes than his opponent.

Of course, I know that development won't happen soon . . . at least not until the powers that be can possibly imagine a world where every vote actually counts!

The first step we must take in order to guarantee that everyone is allowed to exercise their right to vote is to change the timing of elections. Limiting them to 12 hours, with general elections held on a single weekday in November, when weather and/or work often keep many voters away from the polls, was always a bad idea.

The general election must be moved to a time of year when the weather is milder, such as early October or late September, and elections must be held when more working people can get to the polls, such as a Saturday or a Sunday. The length of time for voting must also be expanded to at least 24 hours, or even better, 24-hour access to the polls over a liberal week-end, say, Friday morning to sometime Monday. In fact, allowing 24-hour access to the polls during an entire week would be the best way to guarantee that people who work odd days or shifts can exercise their rightful access to the voting booth.

Of course, in the world I imagine, those ubiquitous community centers in every neighborhood would be ideal polling places, for those who choose to vote in person instead of voting by mail or internet--another convenience that would be available in my concept. But until any of those developments occur, most of my ideas on this subject would work now with little trouble--other than the will to improve the situation for all voters.

The only way to guarantee that all votes are counted accurately is to implement a truly verifiable voting system. While lawmakers and judges continue to stumble in the darkness as they debate the issue of whether voting machines should have a paper receipt, I suggest that they must take the process another step beyond that and set up a system that will guarantee that no candidate will ever have to request a recount again.

Electronic touch machines should be installed in every polling place in the entire country, along with printers that produce two hard copies for every vote cast. Voters would keep one copy so they can see that their choices were actually recorded, and the other would go to a data-entry operator who would key these votes into a different system. With votes recorded in two separate systems, totals can be run on an hourly basis to make sure the two separate electronic records balance. Any time a conflict arises, the paper tickets can be the final authority for balancing a batch of votes.

Incidentally, internet voting could be implemented the same way. Voters would print two copies at a web page which clearly instructs them to do so, and a printer at the server (polling) end would automatically print copies as votes come in. Voters would mail one copy to the elections office, and the votes would be keyed into the second system for the verifying balance. Eventually, these internet votes received both electronically and by mail could be tallied and balanced with each other, again preventing the need for a recount on behalf of any candidate.

To assure accuracy, the job of tallying each system's records could be managed by members of different political parties, and representatives of at least two opposition parties could monitor a polling operation at any time--as long as that type of political division continues to exist. This balanced approach would guarantee that no one could get away with programming a system to rig an election, as many suspect might have occurred during recent elections. The point of this dual-record plan is to provide a fail-safe system and prevent errors from ever cropping up again.

Finally, this country must abolish the anti-democratic institution known as the Electoral College. Traditionalists consider anything the Founding Fathers did to be sacrosanct, but I must remind them that this wrinkle was devised as part of a nascent system that, for most of its history, has denied suffrage to large groups of its citizens. The white male property owners who set up the American government openly declared that the Electoral College was meant to be a tool to prevent the working class from gaining as much political power as the wealthy class that continues to control this nation. It also gave southern states an unfair advantage by allowing extra electoral votes (and seats in the House of Representatives) to represent the huge block of slaves--on the basis of three votes for every five slaves--who couldn't vote in the first place.

While the question of the fairness of the College, if not its constitutionality, has long been discussed, the principle of "one man, one vote" was firmly established as a legal precedent when Jimmy Carter was first elected to the Georgia State Senate in 1962, a landmark decision that President Carter details in his book, *Turning Point* (Three Rivers Press, 1993).

While the Electoral College doesn't give a single vote to each district, as did the old "county unit" system, it is so unbalanced that its legal demise should be a foregone conclusion--if only someone with the power to do so would bring up the question before the national legislature, or at least the courts. Then, and only then, would Americans be able to elect a president in true democratic fashion, with no fear of being outvoted by this terrible specter of the past!

These ideas are directed toward the election process itself, but the elections of 2000 and 2004 also shed a harsh light on several of the old "dirty" tricks that are still being used to keep many minority voters from casting their votes. In the following section on universal suffrage, I discuss some of those problems and offer some solutions.

UNIVERSAL SUFFRAGE

In the previous section on making votes count, I introduced several ideas to help solve some of the problems inherent in our electoral system. But recent elections were infamous for another problem that is a shameful remnant of the past: numerous instances of legal authorities pulling "dirty" tricks to prevent minority citizens from voting.

These problems received so much attention in 2000 that some improvements were made by 2004, but it wasn't enough.

We still have a long way to go. Some things were better in 2004, but some of the "solutions" actually proved to be troublesome themselves, and even more problems from 2004 are coming to light every day. My hope is that this discussion will spark ideas from others that will help us to hold truly democratic elections one day in which everyone has completely unhindered access to the voting booth--and their votes are counted accurately the first time!

According to reports from the 2000 election, in several minority areas in a large midwestern city, polls were closed exactly at 7:00 p.m., in spite of the fact that hundreds of people who'd stopped off after work were still waiting in line to vote!

In an infamous case, a state election official struck names from the voter rolls shortly before the election, claiming they were felons who'd lost their voting rights. It turned out that most of the people were not felons, but they did live in predominantly minority neighborhoods. The worst thing is, none of them even heard about this violation of their civil rights until they reached their polling places on Election Day, where they were actually barred from even being able to cast a provisional ballot!

(Incidentally, an official in the same state tried to do the same thing in 2004 but was stopped in time. One would hope that it didn't occur on such a large scale as was done in the previous election. Unfortunately, information is surfacing even as I'm editing this manuscript that indicates the problem might not only have been worse in 2004 but could have been generated from the highest levels of government!)

Another problem occurred in the same state when Highway Patrol officers set up roadblocks in minority neighborhoods so they could stop people on their way to vote. According to reports, they succeeded in preventing a number of people from being able to reach their polling places, most of which were only a block away from these illegal barriers!

Every one of these problems could have been prevented with a little foresight, something which the authorities didn't see fit to apply in 2000--or didn't want to! But now that such a bright light has been focused on them, the time has come for legislators to establish strict guidelines to prevent any violations from occurring in future elections.

Greater emphasis on internet and absentee voting would ease congestion at polling places, especially at certain times of day, and my suggestion to expand the time, and especially the number of days, that polling places are kept open would really help working people. And with the proliferation of dependable long-distance data transmission, there's no reason a registered voter can't cast a ballot at any polling place that is more convenient to their personal daily schedule, instead of being required to vote only at the polling place nearest their home.

No matter where people go to vote, everyone who reaches the doors to a polling place by the time the polls are scheduled to be closed should be allowed to vote, even if the facility must continue operating for an indefinite length of time past the scheduled closing time. There should also be no locking of the doors early and turning away anyone who arrives just before the scheduled poll closing. If the cutoff time is officially 7:00 p.m., then anyone who joins the end of the line at 6:59 p.m. must be allowed to vote!

The problem of people being incorrectly struck from the voter rolls could be prevented by setting a deadline, such as six months before an election. After the deadline, election officials could not arbitrarily remove any name from the voting roster. When any name is to be removed, for whatever reason, election officials must notify the person by registered letter which requires a return receipt. A month later, a second letter should be sent to anyone whose signed receipt has not been returned. Finally, someone should track down anyone whose receipt still hasn't come back. Such a thorough system would minimize the kind of problems that illegally prevented so many people from voting in 2000, and probably in 2004 as well.

In rare cases where people with voter registration cards are not on the roster, they should be allowed to cast ballots with a code designating their votes as pending a legal appeal on their eligibility. Their votes would constitute the filing of that appeal, which should be heard during the week following the election. That should allow time for appeals to be decided so that legitimate votes could be included in the final tally before the Election Commission certifies the results of the election.

The third violation in question was more complicated, since many people were so frightened by the illegal harassment at official-looking roadblocks that they never made it to their polling places. My suggestion to extend the hours, and especially the number of days, of voting would help, since it would be difficult for these illegal roadblocks to be maintained for very long without being reported--and busted!

I would also suggest that any charges of that type of harassment should be heard by the courts immediately after an election, and anyone who can prove they were denied the right to vote by illegal means should be allowed to cast a late vote which would be added to the final total. Moreover, any public official found to have illegally attempted to prevent any citizen from voting should be dismissed immediately and ordered to pay a severe penalty for the civil-rights violation. More to the point, such people should never again be allowed to serve in any capacity in which they have that kind of influence over the rights of other people. That means there would be a lifetime ban against their ever holding another official government position again!

Some part of these ideas were actually implemented in 2004; for instance, the use of provisional ballots by people whose voting status was in question. But as usual, there were still problems. You can see how difficult it is to stay above the fray on this issue. But if we don't prevent these problems from occurring in the first place, I can only envision a perpetuation of the eternal battles that will not end until complete reform is implemented in our electoral system. Obviously, the people who can implement these changes must focus their imagination and creativity on the situation.

It would be great if they did, but I don't imagine it's going to happen very soon!

Chapter 7

Establishing True Democracy

PRACTICING DEMOCRACY

So far in this book I've detailed several steps that governments could take in order to begin serving all the needs of every citizen, not merely the demands of a favored few. Still, it's important to note that the momentum for these changes must come from citizens themselves. That's because a true democracy is exactly as President Abraham Lincoln described it: "government of the people, by the people, for the people."

The sad thing is, such a government has never actually existed, not even here in the United States. A government that is truly for the people cannot tolerate such societal failures as the millions of people, especially so many children, doomed to wallow in poverty, suffering from malnutrition, often homeless, with so much of their basic needs unmet. In a true democracy, every person would have sufficient food and shelter, access to quality medical care, enough education to be a productive citizen, and much, much more.

The challenge, then, is to establish a system in which the lowest-paid full-time worker earns at least twice as much as it would cost to purchase all the basic goods and services needed to enjoy a dignified existence. And the best resource available to help reach that goal is every member of society. The plan, therefore, must be to empower every citizen to become actively involved in the efforts to reach that goal throughout the world.

But what exactly would that mean? How do people participate in a truly democratic society? There are several steps which define democratic action:

SPEAK UP!

Good citizens identify problems and, where possible, offer solutions, and not just for themselves. They pay attention to what their neighbors need and take steps to get help for them.

In my plan, the primary forum for addressing these needs would be the neighborhood community center, and the first people to approach about problems would be members of the local committee and sub-committee, as described in the chapter on Administering a Peaceful Planet. That would mean a minimum of nine professionals--at least three on the local committee and at least six on the supporting sub-committee--would be available for consultation to the residents of each community of any size.

In addition, since people do have needs at any time of the day or night, at least two people would be required to be on duty at the community center at any given time, 24 hours a day. The night crew would consist of at least one committee or sub-committee member, along with another trained community-service worker.

In the community center, besides small rooms and

offices that would be used for private consultation with individuals, a larger room would be reserved for public meetings, where general problems could be discussed with committee and sub-committee members and other citizens who choose to participate in the discussions. Formal community meetings should be scheduled several times a week, at various times throughout the day and evening, so that any citizen would have ample opportunity to participate in the process. Committee and sub-committee members would make sure that any situation not easily resolved will be discussed at each meeting until a solution is found and implemented.

ACT!

As I emphasize often in this book, the best way to establish an effective democracy would be for each member of the community to contribute a few hours of community service each week. If everyone did that, not only would they be helping their neighbors, they'd be helping to build a system that would provide them with help if and when they need it too!

Serving the community means helping where it is needed most. Perhaps an older or disabled person needs help with daily chores, a homebound person needs a friendly visit now and again, or the 24-hour child-care center that serves all local families needs responsible adult eyes in the playground for an hour or two. In the world I imagine, citizens would advise the community-center staff whenever they or someone they know has a particular need, and citizens would volunteer through the center for a particular assignment for which they are particularly qualified.

Committee and sub-committee members would maintain a list of the tasks that need doing in the community, so citizens would be directed toward the most effective place where they would be of use to their neighbors. Obviously, not everyone can do every job. Tasks should be assigned that match, or at least come close to, each person's skills and talents. Efficient and satisfying public service means balancing what each person does well and enjoys doing with the type of service that is actually needed in the community.

VOTE!

A close relationship with the local community-center staff would help citizens recognize the most important qualification for office: a dedication to helping every person in need. In addition, since every citizen would dedicate a few hours of service to the community each week, more people might decide to dedicate their lives to helping people on a full-time basis, whether it be their own neighbors or people who live in other parts of the world.

Just imagine, if everyone on the planet actually had everything they needed and at least something extra to make their life more enjoyable, then they would be much more likely to believe in the democratic system and to participate in positive ways. And with no shortage of qualified people to run for the public offices where decisions are made that affect people's lives, there would be a greater likelihood that governments would work toward peaceful solutions that work for everyone, instead of implementing policies that primarily benefit the favored few.

RIGHTS AND RESPONSIBILITIES

Back in the early 1970s, when airport security was a bare nod to a rash of overseas hijackings, a grandmother with an impish sense of humor passed through a San

Antonio metal detector and picked up her purse as it rolled out of the x-ray machine. With a twinkle in her eye, she turned to the guard and boldly declared, "Well, I guess you didn't find my pocketknife!"

Before she could take another step toward the gate, another guard was brusquely escorting her to a security office some distance away. No amount of protests could convince him to let her catch her plane while he filled out forms reporting her behavior, and she was finally forced to take a later flight. Of course, his deeper intent was to give her time to consider the seriousness of her words.

When my mother-in-law finally arrived in Denver, she explained the reason for the delay, ending in typical fashion with, "I was so mad, I could eat a banana!"

It took us a while to convince her of the wisdom of the law against saying certain things to airport personnel. She finally admitted, grudgingly, that she should have thought twice before playing another of her famous practical jokes.

Momma's experience demonstrates a vital aspect of the nature of freedom: Every right must be perfectly balanced with an equal responsibility. With freedom of speech and the press come the stipulation that our words, actions, and ideas not harm others. Besides avoiding incendiary speech, at least in certain situations, and abusive language, it is illegal to spread lies about someone, either by mouth (slander) or in print (libel).

Similar caveats attach to the other freedoms listed in the first two amendments of the Bill of Rights. The charge to separate the institutions of church and state marked the first time in history that a government acknowledged that while everyone has the right to worship as they please, no person or group has the right to impose their beliefs on others. The First Amendment specifically states that people have a right to assemble, as long as it's done "peaceably," and the rights to petition the government for a redress of grievances and to bear arms come with heavy responsibilities that these actions not inflict harm on either governments or other citizens.

This means we all have a duty to protect these rights, along with all those detailed in subsequent constitutional amendments and civil rights laws, for every member of society. During Word War II, President Franklin Delano Roosevelt demarcated the range of human rights in his speech on the "Four Freedoms": freedom of speech and expression, freedom to worship God in one's own way, freedom from want, and freedom from fear. He ended his explanation of each freedom by saying it must be protected "everywhere in the world," not merely in the United States.

Given these basic principles of humanity, no government should tolerate unemployment, hunger, homelessness--or any of the numerous conditions which condemn people to an existence that is no better than slavery. Yet, even as many sincere people struggle to improve these conditions for themselves, their family members, and their neighbors, most admit that the problems are too complex to be solved by spending time and money in the same old ways.

The solution can only be found through a systemic and systematic approach, by removing the complexities that now tie our hands, addressing the underlying causes of all these social ills, and building a system which solves these problems and prevents them from ever cropping up again.

That's why I'm suggesting that the only way to totally eliminate poverty is to establish a system in which the lowest-paid full-time worker earns at least twice as much as it would cost to purchase all the basic goods and services needed to enjoy a dignified existence. This can only be done by empowering individuals and communities around the world to share resources with every other community, so that we will all be able to help everyone reach this goal on a worldwide basis.

A vital aspect of that work is the duty of each person to contribute some effort toward building a truly democratic society in which everyone's rights are absolutely respected. That means we must not only refrain from doing anything that brings harm to others, we must also speak up when we see harm being done to someone else and, if possible, do all that we can to prevent it from happening in the first place.

That's the reason I've written this book--and continue to write about the issues discussed here--in the hope that humans might one day turn away from the destructive path we've traveled throughout history. It is past time to begin building a society in which every human being's basic civil rights are absolutely respected, where poverty is only a distant memory and peace prevails all around the world.

Like my mother-in-law, I don't always know when to keep quiet. But I do try to approach the topics from a positive point of view, to offer hope for others, and to suggest creative solutions for the many problems I see around me. My only regret is that Marjorie Jordan didn't live long enough to see how much her daughter-in-law is carrying on that legacy of free speech.

69

Chapter 8

Universal Education

LEARNING PROBLEMS

As much as I love both convenience and salads-- with the flavors of different veggies in each bite-- I'm not a fan of those salads that are stored and sold in plastic bags. When produce vegetate together in plastic, flavors tend to blend. Lettuce doesn't taste like lettuce so much as a mutant: part carrot, a dash of celery, and a bit of whatever else that poor lettuce cohabits with. The pieces lose their distinctive flavors so that lettuce, tomato, and carrot turn into a blended taste you might call "letomrot."

I feel the same way about the "vegetable stew" flavor of mixed vegetables and the homogenized odor of flowers that mingle with bunches of other buds in florists' fridges. And I'm no fan of the lock-step, homogeneous approach that most schools take in educating the masses for our modern society.

I'm certainly not alone. For decades, a host of experts

have complained about the American educational system. They note that it doesn't really educate many students, especially those who drop out early from sheer boredom and frustration, or those who are passed along through each grade and graduated--even though they can barely read.

Many of those who do master the curriculum come away with little more than the standard data they were spoon-fed over the years, and many don't even retain much of that, no doubt because of the way in which it's being taught. Most go into the world only to repeat the mistakes of their predecessors in business, government, and society because they've never been challenged to find innovative ways to solve problems. And many of the brightest kids fail classes because they're bored to tears, drop out before they get their high-school diplomas, and waste their lives in jobs that barely tap their many talents.

Sadly, this is the inevitable result of a system that stifles creativity and discourages original thinking while force-feeding canned lessons to students at a predetermined pace that fails to address individual needs, interest, or ability to comprehend the material.

Instead of injecting challenges and creative thinking into the learning experience, authorities recently imposed a so-called "no child left behind" policy that emphasizes test-taking over learning, turning students into robots who regurgitate pre-packaged data that has little to do with the life they'll lead as adults.

Schools are not only letting down students, they're shortchanging society as a whole. The only solution is to take an honest look at the way schools are generally being run now and devise the changes that must be implemented to turn them into centers of enlightenment that spark everyone in the community to appreciate education as one of the great experiences in a fulfilling life. To do that, we must understand why problems exist in the first place.

Did you know that the modern American system of public education was based on the assembly line model by a team of industrialists headed by the man who introduced that principle into manufacturing, Henry Ford? Of course, they borrowed heavily from the German system that had been developed for a single purpose: to turn out workers who would be ideally suited for employment in modern factories, as well as filling government jobs where unified thinking was the norm.

The only bow to students' individual abilities was the process of separating the brightest from the rest of pack for college preparation, while those with "average" abilities were encouraged to "learn a trade," such as woodworking or mechanics for the boys and nursing or teaching for the girls. As a result, high schools turned out thousands of people who spent their lives installing seats in cars as they rolled down assembly lines, while colleges produced engineers who designed new automobile models every year.

They weren't looking for people who could devise grand solutions to serious social problems. Instead, they espoused Charles Erwin Wilson's axiom: "What is good for the country is good for General Motors, and what's good for General Motors is good for the country."

That's why individual initiative and creativity aren't high on the list of educational priorities, and students are segregated into classes by age rather than ability and fed a core curriculum at a predetermined rate. They're expected to learn the same way cars are built, with parts delivered according to a preset schedule and everyone moving along the treadmill at the same pace--with little or no consideration given to a student's individual strengths or weaknesses.

Another problem can be found in the strong emphasis being put on education in science and math. At the same time, little or no attention is being made to the great need to train highly intelligent and creative people in such vital areas as sociology and political science so they can develop solutions to the global problems that threaten the very existence of the planet--many of which were caused by an over-reliance on science, without applying conscience in every decision.

On the other hand, in the world I imagine, schools would be managed in a completely different fashion. No longer would classes be arranged according to an artificial age-grade level. In fact, organized classes would constitute only a small part of a vibrant multimedia system of learning that would benefit people of all ages, serve everyone in the community, and train intelligent and creative workers who would not only serve their employers and their neighbors but work hard to improve the situation for businesses and people around the world.

Such a system would not only train better workers, it would produce citizens who would help build a world in which the lowest-paid full-time worker is able to earn at least twice as much as it would cost to purchase all the basic goods and services needed to enjoy a dignified existence. In the learning model I imagine, access to all educational resources according to individual capacity would be a vital part of the basic services that each person would receive.

Such an educational system would finally train people to the limits of their abilities and encourage their creativity and initiative so they will be able to put an end to poverty throughout the world and build a truly peaceful society on the entire planet, for the first time in history.

INDIVIDUAL LEARNING

In the previous section on learning problems, I discussed several aspects of the current educational model that, I believe, hinder the system's ability to help many students become creative and productive members of a truly peaceful and democratic society. In this section, I'll share some ideas for turning education into a lifelong process to equip every citizen for the work of fashioning the world I imagine: a society in which poverty is only a distant memory and peace is the norm.

One of the most important ways in which my plan differs from the current model is the absence of age-grade class divisions. Instead of advancing in all subjects at a prescribed rate, students would be allowed to progress in each subject at their own pace. Some might zip through required math lessons while getting the extra help they need to understand grammar and spelling. Conversely, others might flourish on their own in language studies while they need extra help to understand the basic principles of math.

Besides attending some classes in their neighborhood schools, all students everywhere would have access to a wide range of study materials, from traditional books and workbooks to recordings and internet sites that would give them access to the knowledge and wisdom of the best educators in the world. The most valuable tool for many students would be the personal help they need to advance in their weakest subjects which they would receive from tutors of any age who master those subjects easily. And the same students who need tutoring in their weak areas could return the favor in the subjects they do well in for others who need that kind of help.

Of course, personal tutoring would be just one of the

many services that qualified ordinary citizens could provide for their neighbors, as explained in the community service section of the chapter on Administering a Peaceful Planet. And everyone would be paid for this work. Even the young people would receive similar remuneration for helping their fellow students. In the age and disability section of the chapter on Universal Employment, I discussed my plan to ensure that people of all ages would receive all the basic necessities, and at least a little more, in exchange for their labors, with the amount of labor they contribute for that basic compensation to be based upon their age and/or physical and mental capacities.

Another major difference between the current educational model and the one I imagine would be the lack of required class attendance. Classes would be held every day of the week at schools in every community, but students wouldn't have to attend every class to receive credit for that course, since they would have many tools to help them master the course material. The exception would be a subject in which on-site work is a required part of the lesson plan, as with a lab course, for instance.

A vital tool for implementing this plan would be the class recording system. All classes would be digitally recorded. Students who attend classes would be able to use these recordings later to review the material as needed, while students who watch the classes from another location in real time via the internet could participate in class activities to the extent they can. All class recordings would be available over the internet to schools and students throughout the world, so everyone could benefit from the best teachers and classes, no matter where classes are held or students are located.

Few classes would be limited to the 45- or 55-minute models that are the norm in schools today. With most classes ranging from one-and-a-half to three hours each, students could give greater attention to each subject and take all the time they need to understand more complicated material. All instructors would be assisted by adults and/or students with some qualification in those subjects, thus easing the team leader's burden of teaching and grading papers and tests. In fact, teachers wouldn't have to waste any of their valuable professional time monitoring students' testing. That task could be handled by almost any trustworthy person, usually an adult, as part of their community service.

Another way in which average citizens would contribute to the educational system would be by mentoring students and overseeing their course requirements. For instance, a mentor could help a student plan a personal learning schedule, including class attendance and individual study programs, or check on a student's mastery of particular subjects. The mentor's duties could range from listening to a young person read for a little while each day to helping a teenager search for resources on an obscure subject.

In the next section on testing knowledge, I'll discuss more ways in which schools all over the world would help train people to participate in a thriving world market in which the lowest-paid full-time worker on the planet is able to earn at least twice as much as it would cost to purchase all the basic goods and services needed to enjoy a dignified existence.

These schools would also provide citizens with the wisdom and tools they could use to build and maintain a truly democratic and peaceful society, for the first time in history.

USEFUL LEARNING

In the previous section on individual learning, I

77

introduced several ideas that could help the educational system concentrate more resources on each student while easing the burden on the hardest working members of that system, the teachers. Though I discussed some unconventional applications, multimedia systems in use now could be expanded to provide universal access to any textbook, workbook, or other educational tool that students need to pursue their goals. All that's really needed is the political and social will to make that happen.

In the world I imagine, universal educational access would be the norm, not the exception. And since experts acknowledge that different people learn various skills in markedly different ways, the universal availability of instructor training and teaching materials in any discipline would ensure that everyone has a chance to learn the skills they need to help build a truly democratic and peaceful society.

But all these resources won't make much difference to many students unless two aspects of the current educational model are completely overhauled: testing and certification.

In the current system, almost all students are tested and scored the same way, and score averages are used to rate the quality of a school's teaching methods. Unfortunately, the practice has several inherent flaws.

Administering standardized tests to every student in the same way, and usually at the same time, guarantees that a significant number will fail. Many students lack the skills to perform in the standard testing medium, while others have profound disabilities that school administrators often fail to address. Students who don't read well, for instance, do poorly on written tests, though they can usually prove their knowledge of a subject with an oral test. Many know the material well but freeze up during tests. Still others might never be able to master certain subjects because of severe learning disabilities.

In the world I imagine, students would be tested in many different ways, according to their individual needs and abilities. Some would take written tests, including the ubiquitous multiple-choice, along with essay questions that force them to think more deeply and express themselves clearly. Those who don't read or write well would take oral tests, even as they receive extra tutoring to improve their reading and writing skills to the limit of their capacities. And each student's test results would be used to develop individual study and tutoring plans in areas where they need extra support.

But all this testing does little to measure a student's preparedness for the real world. My plan includes another big change that would help young people learn more about many of the personal and professional situations they'll face as adults.

In industrialized countries, most young people attend school full time, and many also hold part-time minimum-wage jobs. With homework and extracurricular activities, they have little chance to study the wide range of employment opportunities available so that they can make informed career choices, and few learn such practical skills as balancing a checkbook, investing money wisely, or strengthening interpersonal relationships.

In my plan, education in real-world topics would begin at a young age, with books and workshops that teach small children about the duties of people with different jobs, how to make a shopping list, spend money carefully, and put extra money in the bank. As students grow and advance in these areas, their tools would become more sophisticated, and every student would be required to spend some time each day on at least one of these personal-development subjects.

Information would be presented in several formats. Young children would use activity and coloring books and "play" grocery store with toy store-models, plastic products to "buy," and play "money" to "pay" for these items. Later, the same students would embark on school-sponsored shopping trips so they can gain real-world experience buying simple things for themselves and their families. Older students would benefit from more complicated lessons, videos, and workshops with speakers from a wide range of professions and trades. By this time, most would be learning how to manage their own checking, savings, credit, and investment accounts.

With my plan, by the time students enter their teens, they would also spend some learning time each week actually working in trades or professions that they might like to practice later on. These temporary jobs could last from a few hours to several weeks, or even longer. Besides gaining insight into what each job entails, young people would make personal contacts for the future and earn extra money as well--because in the world I imagine, every bit of labor would be rewarded with real money, not merely a "thank you" and a handshake!

In the next section on learning to work, I'll explain how the connection between schools and businesses would help train people for any job they'll ever need while providing employers with a rich pool of well-trained workers.

Of course, another way that every young person would gain on-the-job training would be by doing work in their communities, helping neighbors and earning money to buy all the basic goods and services they need to enjoy a dignified existence.

With such a wide range of educational resources available, young people around the world would be equipped to help build a society where poverty is non-existent, a world that is truly democratic and peaceful, for the first time in history.

LEARNING TO WORK

In the previous section on useful learning, I introduced my idea that in the world I imagine, young people would incorporate short-term jobs at different companies into their overall program of learning. This part of my plan would accomplish several things at once.

The time they spend in different industries would give young people more insight to help them choose their future careers, as well as contacts to help them with job searches. Since their time at each company would be split between observing people in different jobs and performing simpler tasks themselves, students would develop many skills, including good work habits. Students would be paid for the time they actually work, as noted in the previous section, and their job performance ratings from employers and fellow workers would be entered into their school records. Even better, young people who discover the careers they want to pursue as adults can continue to labor in those areas while the employers can mentor them through the rest of their school years and into their early adult years.

Exposing young people to various jobs during their school years demonstrates a vital aspect of my plan for a more effective education, since the only way to make a truly informed choice of career is to become as well informed on all available choices as possible.

This principle should apply to other aspects of education as well. That's why I propose that besides being tested and graded in their regular academic classes, each student should be encouraged to spend time informally studying and auditing classes on many different subjects. This practice would not only expose students to a wider range of knowledge than they'd glean from their required courses, it would help them develop the habit of absorbing data in many subjects that might come in handy later.

One area where this habit would be especially useful is the arts, especially music. Currently, children usually study an instrument as if it will become a lifelong pursuit. In rare cases, this approach leads to a valuable education and a successful career. But for many young people, the experience turns out to be either an interesting diversion from their other studies or, in too many cases, a grueling exercise that steals time from things they actually prefer to be doing.

While I believe music is an important part of a well-rounded education, I also feel children should not be forced into playing any instrument the way they are often made to do now. That's why, in my plan, all young people would be exposed to various types of music. For most, this exposure would be short-term and informal, but all students would approach the subject from three angles: by listening to different types of music, reading about or listening to lectures on the principles of music and composition, and trying out different instruments for different periods of time to see if they enjoy playing any of them.

For most students, the point of this exercise would not be to get a grade but to gain experience and widen their horizons. With this approach, music would be less of an academic burden and more of an enjoyable pastime, even a break from their more serious academic duties. By requiring every child to devote time each week to this discipline, many who wouldn't recognize a musical inclination might eventually take up an instrument that they only intended to try out for a short time. A few might discover a talent that would be overlooked in the present system because of a lack of exposure to a wide range of musical disciplines and instruments.

Exposing young people to art and drama in the same fashion would introduce them to many things they often don't study now. For instance, presenting various interpretations of the works of Shakespeare in a leisurely forum, rather than as a graded course, would encourage more students to appreciate his genius, and those who really want to do so can study the works of the Bard for credit.

To round out my points in the previous sections of this chapter, my academic plan would include testing and grading only for required courses and for those which an individual student needs for the type of certification that matches their personal educational and employment plans and goals. And since testing would be supervised by trained community workers instead of teachers, students could take tests for any course at any time that is convenient to them. That factor would help many students do better on tests, since the current strict test-taking regimen often forces students to test at times when they can't perform well, as when they are ill or before they've been able to fully master the data in their weaker subjects.

In my plan, certification would also be less rigid than it is now. This doesn't mean lowering the requirements for standard diplomas or degrees; in fact, the requirements in each area could actually be tougher when students are allowed to advance at their own pace in their best subjects and get help in areas where they need it. But a wider certification range would also give people with certain learning disabilities a tool to demonstrate their workplace abilities to employers in specific areas where they are strongest, though they might not qualify for a diploma certifying their mastery of the wider range of subjects required for most forms of traditional education.

In the next section on learning for life, I'll discuss my plan to make education a lifelong habit for everyone. And with greater educational opportunities, including a wide range of certification for even the weakest students, in the world I imagine everyone would have the opportunity to become much better equipped to do their part to help build a society with no poverty that is truly democratic and peaceful.

LEARNING FOR LIFE

So far, I've concentrated on the nuts and bolts of educating young people, but for years it's been common for adults to attend school as well. Many are dropouts who want to get their high-school diplomas or even college degrees, and others are laid-off workers who need skills to find jobs in new areas. A third group consists of people who simply love to learn or want to earn advanced degrees.

Besides adding to their store of knowledge, these people are improving their health and lengthening their lives. They are living proof that using the brain is the best exercise one can get. That's why in the world I imagine, not only would education at all levels be considered a basic necessity and, therefore, available to everyone around the world, a minimum amount of continued learning would actually be required for people of all ages.

This exercise in mental improvement would range from the academic to the arts to physical education, and everyone would be encouraged to vary their experiences. For instance, a person might study calculus one winter, take a folk-dancing class in spring, then study oil painting in the summer. Like younger students, adults could alternate organized classes with informal personal study, proceeding at their own pace in each subject. They could earn credits in various subjects and take tests whenever they decide to do so.

Since age would no longer be a factor in school groups, even at the earliest levels, most classes would consist of people of varying ages and experience. Thus, adults who want to bone up on elementary math--especially the "new math" that has most of us older folks so befuddled--or improve reading skills could attend classes that consist of many young students. Since young peoples' schedules would include personal study and part-time work, they could attend any class at any time from morning to night.

Moreover, educational facilities would stay open at all hours of the day and night and throughout the year, with no one taking a break from the school routine for more than two or three weeks at a time. The same would be true of keeping up with the universal responsibility for community service. This would put an end to the September back-to-school slump, when so many young people find it hard to get into the groove and begin studying again after a summer of just so much "goofing off."

In the world I imagine, sports and the arts would also be managed differently from the way they are now. Recently, many schools have cut cultural and sports programs for most students so they can concentrate resources on those who are especially gifted, especially in sports. In my plan, every young person would engage in some type of physical and cultural activities during the day, though they wouldn't necessarily have to be organized like the programs schools still run--or don't anymore so they can save money!

In the section on learning to work, I explained how, in my plan, every student would sample music and other artistic areas for short periods of time as a required part of education in the arts. The same approach should be taken with physical activity. Obviously, only a few people have the talent to get serious about sports, and resources should be provided for those who do, but everyone needs some type of physical activity each day. In my plan, that habit would begin in early childhood, and it would be encouraged and supported for every person of any age in every community throughout the world.

Toward that end, people of all ages, at both school and work, would be able to schedule short breaks for some type of physical activity, from simple walks to informal games with others who also need relief from the daily grind. Even after only 15 minutes of exercise, most people would return to their studies or labors refreshed and ready to concentrate on the tasks at hand.

At least three times a week, everyone who is healthy enough to do so would engage in more concentrated physical activity for half an hour or longer. This plan coincides with current knowledge about physical fitness and training and would provide a good start for youngsters who need to develop the good habits of a healthy lifestyle. This plan would also help people who have problems with hyperactivity, since the frequent breaks they could schedule according to their individual needs would help them to better focus their time and energy in both study and work.

Another educational area where I would mix current programs with more innovative ideas would be in a required class that trains people to make better personal decisions. Too many schools fail to teach students how to handle finances and relationships, and how to effectively participate in their communities. The result is a society with a failing economy and people drowning in debt; severe problems with domestic abuse and a mushrooming divorce rate; and citizens who feel totally disconnected from their neighbors.

On the other hand, in the world I imagine, even very young people would learn how to manage money; they would be trained to practice good manners not only in public but within their own families; and even the youngest would learn that the only way for any of us to feel safe and secure is to take care of people in need in the community. This way everyone would know that they can get the help they need when that time comes.

With this type of training available to all, everyone would have the resources they need to help build a world in which the lowest-paid full-time worker on the planet is able to earn at least twice as much as it would cost to purchase all the basic goods and services necessary for a dignified existence. And with such a good education, everyone would have the skills they need to help build a society that is truly democratic and peaceful, for the first time in history.

Chapter 9

Universal Health Care

HEALTHY LIVING

For years, the United States has lagged behind every other industrialized nation in the world by denying adequate medical care to a large number of its citizens. Worse, recent changes in the Medicare and Medicaid programs, a sharp rise in poor and uninsured working people, and a record national debt make it even harder for most Americans to get the medical care they need. In many places around the country, this nightmare is intensified because many medical facilities, especially emergency rooms, are so overwhelmed and underfunded that they're unable to provide care for many patients--even those with medical insurance!

Obviously, the current political situation will not solve this problem. And though the alternative camp proposes much needed medical-insurance coverage for almost everyone, such a welcome step would still be a mere stop-gap measure in a sea of exploding medical "red ink." The real problem lies in the fact that necessary medical care continues to be treated as a for-profit market commodity instead of a basic service to which every human being has an inherent right, according to their individual needs.

In the world I imagine, the existing fragmented--and expensive--medical industry would be completely overhauled. In my plan, everyone would receive all the healthcare services they need, when they need it. And identifying that "need" will require a more systematic approach than has ever been taken before.

In the first place--unlike the current system where many people have to wait until they're in dire straits before they get help--every measure would be taken to keep people healthy in order to minimize the overall demand for medical care. That means promoting healthy lifestyles, including regular exercise, healthy eating, and cleaning up the environment. I've introduced two of these points in the learning for life section of the chapter on Universal Education (making exercise a lifetime habit) and the jobs, wages, and benefits section of the chapter on Universal Employment (establishing worldwide pollution controls).

While the third goal must be managed on a group basis in every community around the world, the first two require both individual responsibility and community support. Besides teaching everyone healthy living habits, in my plan, communities would provide space and equipment for gyms and sports programs. Each citizen would use the services for a length of time designated for "basic" use. If a person chooses to devote more than the basic time allowance to physical activities when community equipment is available, they would pay an extra fee for this extra time of "general" use. On the other hand, if extended exercise time is part of prescribed therapy for a medical condition, the cost would be included as part of the person's basic medical benefit and the time would be counted as basic use.

Of course, people who are serious about body building or sports might choose to apply an amount equal to the value of their basic workout toward part of the membership charge at a private gym or sports club, then they'd be responsible for any charges above the basic amount allotted to each citizen. This is one example of how a basic allowance could be combined with extra personal payment to cover the higher cost of a private service. Thus, citizens would receive the basic service they need, plus the extra service they want, as detailed in the needs versus wants section in the chapter on Building Peace without Poverty. This principle of combining basic value with extra personal payment could be used to purchase larger or upscale products, including everything from food to vehicles and homes.

In the world I imagine, the next step toward preventing illness would come with approved alternative therapies, such as regular chiropractic adjustments, deep-tissue massage, and herbal supplements. Obviously, not all disciplines are right for everyone, and a certain amount of personal and professional judgment must be applied in making these choices. In fact, allowing alternative therapies as basic services would place a greater burden than exists now for medical authorities to pursue objective research into the benefits of these therapies for healthy people, as well as people who suffer from various medical conditions.

The third step necessary to preventing the need for more expensive medical treatment would be to provide everyone with regular examinations and basic diagnostic testing. Each person's schedule for these services would be set according to their age, physical condition, and family history--*not* individual insurance coverage!

Thus, every woman of a certain age would receive free mammograms every few years, unless her grandmother's breast cancer dictates annual tests that begin at a much earlier age than normal. The same principle would apply if a man has prostate cancer in the family. (Perhaps if that test were "free," he wouldn't be so reluctant to have the procedure done!) And a woman with the slightest indication of heart problems would receive comprehensive cardiac diagnostic testing, instead of being dismissed because of an archaic prejudice that heart disease is a man's disease.

In the next section on the business of health, I'll discuss my ideas for providing medical care to every citizen who needs it, and in the section on give me a break(!) I'll explain how another preventive factor would be an inherent byproduct of the reforms I suggest: the natural reduction of the stress that aggravates, and even triggers, so many of the terrible diseases that plague people all over the world!

Of course, the most important byproduct of improved health care for everyone would be that people around the world would be much better equipped to build a society that is truly democratic and peaceful, for the first time in history.

THE BUSINESS OF HEALTH

In the previous section on healthy living, I detailed some of the steps that can be taken to minimize the need for much of the expensive medical care that is called for now. One of those steps involves timely medical checkups and testing. That means providing everyone with adequate medical services when they can do the most good, which is currently unavailable to a shocking percentage of the population. Worse, this crisis has mushroomed in the last few years, especially in the United States.

During debates on this issue, people on one side of the political spectrum claim that "health insurance is not a right." They're always quick to add their contention that "anybody can walk into any emergency room and get the medical care they need." I've never heard anyone challenge these statements, so I'm going to do so in this forum.

In the section on healthy living, I mentioned the fact that many emergency rooms are so overwhelmed and underfunded that they can no longer provide minimum care for a lot of people, especially the ongoing care that people with chronic conditions require. So I have a couple of questions for the super-tilted pols who claim everything is rosy in Medicine Land:

How many people who believe no one has a right to health insurance are willing to go without their own "inconvenient" medical insurance, that they probably pay barely a pittance for, and just depend on the existing public-health system for their own medical needs--and especially, for their loved ones?

How many people who believe no one has a right to health insurance have spent a single evening just sitting in the waiting room of a major metropolitan emergency room on a normal Saturday night? Not even a holiday--Christmas or New Year's Eve, for instance. Just any old Saturday night!

If the answer to either of these questions is "yes," those prejudiced pols would never make those first two--idiotic!--statements.

Obviously, the lack of health insurance is expensive, not only for people who can't get the medical care they need, but for society as a whole. Sick people are not only a drain on the public coffers because of the cost of their medical care, they're unproductive citizens. At least they're not as productive as they would be if they received the quality of care that they really need, or better yet, had adequate preventive care before they even got sick in the first place.

If you think being sick is no big deal, just think how a serious ongoing medical condition stacks up against those three items that Thomas Jefferson listed in the Declaration of Independence as the fundamentals to which everyone has an inherent right: Life, Liberty, and the Pursuit of Happiness!

Take Life, for example: If you're sick and don't get the medical care you need, you could die--actually lose that Life which is your right!--or at least the quality of that Life is severely compromised.

That's one!

Now for Liberty: How can anyone be free when they are a prisoner of a body that doesn't work well--but which could work better if society respected their right to the health care they need?

Two!

Then there's Pursuit of Happiness: Just try pursuing anything when you're hobbled by untreated injuries or limited by continuing chronic illness, and you can't get the medical care you really need!

Three!

Bingo!

Okay, if medical insurance is not an inherent right, then why can't people get adequate health care, especially timely preventive care, without it?

On the other hand, this problem is not limited to those people who have no health insurance, especially since HMOs and other managed-care "services" got into the act!

In the *New York Times*, Robert Pear reports that the policy to push Medicare patients into PPOs has raised prices while diminishing the quality of health care for senior and disabled citizens ("Private Plans Costing More for Medicare," September 17, 2004; "Inquiry on Medicare Finds Improper Limits on Choices," September 28, 2004; *New York Times*). That means Medicare patients are getting sicker and the rest of us are paying more for that inferior care, while the businesses that are supposed to provide health care are just getting richer while doing a worse job than was done before this plan was adopted!

My favorite "editorial" statement on this situation comes from the movie, "As Good as It Gets," when Helen Hunt makes an unprintable statement which her (new) doctor laughingly interprets as the "technical name" for HMOs! I swear (no pun intended!), something's got to give! And passing more laws that further fatten the coffers of HMOs, drug companies, and other corporations is not the answer.

Now, just imagine what life would be like if everyone were able to get the health care they need, when they need it. Not just emergency care during acute episodes, but diagnostic tests and ongoing treatment for all those medical conditions that could be minimized if only the correct preventive approach were taken to their overall health care.

In the next section on healthy medicine, I'll discuss some ideas I have that might actually cure this medical mess. I don't know if it'll ever happen, but one must continue to dream!

Especially since, without a system that delivers quality health care to every person in the world, we'll never be able to make any progress toward establishing the world I imagine, where the lowest-paid full-time worker on the planet is able to earn at least twice as much as it would cost to purchase all the basic goods and services necessary to enjoy a dignified existence--including health care!

HEALTHY MEDICINE

Have you ever received a letter from your employer-sponsored health-insurance provider that opens with a statement about the company's gratitude that you selected their service, then goes on to express their regret that the test or treatment your doctor prescribed isn't covered by the policy you chose?

I often wonder whether anyone in the insurance industry appreciates the sadistic irony of that form letter! Your money pays the salary of the people whose job is to decide that you won't get the services you're paying for.

That's just one symptom of the health-care crisis in the United States. More and more Americans have no choice regarding the kind of health care they receive, if they even get health care at all. And while less overall service is being delivered, the industry just keeps on getting richer!

The time has come for every American to receive all the medical services they need at reasonable cost. That's why we have to look at where the money is going now and how it should be directed in a fair society. Of course, there is a difference between what can be done now and the ideal world I imagine, where every person receives all necessary health care, including dental and vision services, as part of the basic services I discussed in the needs versus wants section of the chapter on Building Peace without Poverty. For now, I'll just explain steps that could be taken quickly in an effort to clean up the mess the country is mired in now.

I know you'll agree that the first place to cut the cost of

medical care should be the department in every insurance company where people decide that you aren't going to get the care you pay for. Eliminating the expense of operating those departments would undoubtedly pay for a lot of the tests and treatments that aren't covered now because of the decisions that are made in those offices.

Then there should be a cap put on the total amount of cash and perks paid to every executive in the entire health-care industry, say, at a million dollars in today's money for the top guy in each company. And lesser lights on the executive ladder would receive salaries descending along a well-regulated scale below that million.

I have nothing against anybody making a profit for hard work, except when companies cut necessary patient care for people who have little or nothing so they can pay more money and benefits to people who already have more than they'll ever need in ten lifetimes. In the world I imagine, any company that delivers basic goods or services could not be structured that way, but for now, health-care companies must put the goal of delivering services at reasonable cost above the quest for profit, both personal and corporate.

This means changing corporate structure and shedding profit-hungry investors. Many companies might withdraw from the industry altogether, which wouldn't be so bad, since every layer of administration sucks more money out of the system. Those that remain would do so for reasons more noble than greed, and shrinking the industry would lessen the risk that makes the business so cutthroat now.

I propose that all health-care companies switch from the public-stock model, which is so easily manipulated for profit, to a more stable bond system that provides a less volatile return based entirely on gross sales receipts. No accounting tricks, no phantom divisions or partnerships, only money the company actually earns in exchange for products and/or services actually produced and delivered. Companies must be extremely careful about unnecessary expenses. Waste diminishes operating budgets, inhibits the quality of service, and limits the chances for real growth. And as closely as public companies are--or should be--regulated, government oversight must be more stringent for companies that deliver such vital basic services as health care.

One of the easiest ways to slash the cost of health care would be to eliminate advertising. There was never a good reason for this expensive practice, which tends to confuse consumers much more than it informs them, at least the way it's used as a selling tool now.

The best way to provide information about people and companies that provide health services is through well-regulated universal databases. For instance, a physician directory would report every licensed health provider's name, address, phone number, education, experience, professional philosophy, etc. Those information agencies that now provide services to member doctors could be expanded to include all doctors within certain parameters, such as geographic regions, and the same could be done for entities in every area of the health-care industry.

The most vital data that must be included in these databanks would be a medical provider's complete legal history. We also need a worldwide licensing system with a strict policy of "three strikes and you never practice again--anywhere on the planet"! This might sound harsh, but there are plenty of useful ways for a failed doctor to contribute to society without risking the lives of innocent patients. Besides, such a universal licensing policy would virtually eliminate the reason for most lawsuits, thus reducing the overall cost of health care.

Patient records should also be compiled in electronic form so medical professionals would no longer order redundant and wasteful tests and treatments. Such an electronic record would also enable medical case managers to oversee the confusing journey through the medical maze for anyone dealing with severe injury or chronic illness.

Finally, insurance companies--at least while they continue to insist on keeping their greedy little fingers in the health-care pie--must establish a uniform system of claim filing and benefit payments that addresses the medical needs of every patient rather than the selfish demands of profit-hungry executives and corporations! This means they must cover the cost of care for people with pre-existing medical conditions and those who require experimental treatments.

We will only have a truly healthy medical industry when every person in the world can get health care when they actually need it, without jumping through administrative hoops or breaking their personal piggy bank to get it.

GIVE ME A BREAK!

When I talk with people in the health-care industry and the conversation turns to the high turnover in such vital areas as nursing and emergency response, I mention my belief that people who work in high-stress professions should be allowed to take regular breaks from their most intense duties by performing lower-stress desk jobs for at least a few weeks each year.

For instance, nurses could fill in for people in the hospital's administrative department while the desk-jockeys are on vacation, and after a week or two everyone would return to their regular duties with renewed vigor. Even better, there'd be less chance that so many nurses would abandon the profession altogether because the only time they get a break from the stress now is when they take their own vacations.

The key to this plan would be that these paid work-breaks from the worst stress of the regular job would pose no risk to a professional's place on the career track, as often happens now when people experience "burnout" because they can't handle the incessant stress of their jobs.

Stress--at least a reduction of the bad kind, "distress"-- is a vital part of my plan for the world I imagine, especially since too much of that bad stress is the cause of so many of the problems that are so rampant in our world now. But that doesn't mean a productive world would be completely without stress. In fact, the beneficial type of stress, known as "eustress," often acts as a spur to help people work toward their goals.

The trouble is, the same factor that acts as a positive spur to one person can have an extremely negative effect on another person. That's why, in the world I imagine, everyone would be able to control these factors in their own lives so they'd have all the tools they need to accomplish what they want, including the type of encouragement they need to help them reach their goals.

Of course, the easiest way to eliminate a great deal of the distress in our current society is to ensure that everyone has access to all the basic goods and services they need to enjoy a dignified existence at a price equal to no more than half the amount earned by the lowest-paid full-time worker on the planet.

Imagine, if no one had to worry whether they'd be able to pay the mortgage, go to the doctor when they need to, or feed their children if they lost their job. How much easier all our lives would be if each of us did our part to make sure everyone has what they need, as I've discussed in every chapter throughout this book.

These reforms are within the control of human society. They are problems of policy, not chance. We humans might not always be able to protect ourselves from the destructive power of nature, but we can work together to establish a system that provides everyone with all the basic goods and services they need in exchange for their contribution to a well-functioning society.

What's more, reducing the distress that controls so much of our lives today would make it easier for members of a reformed society to respond to everyone's basic needs. For instance, much of the illness that now contributes to the mushrooming cost of medical care is aggravated, and often triggered, by stress. If society eliminated many of the factors that are now making people so sick, then the need for so much medical care--and, thus, the cost of that care--would be greatly diminished.

Other social ills would also be affected in positive ways, such as the high rates of spousal and child abuse, alcoholism and drug addiction, crime and, perhaps not surprisingly, terrorism. After all, if society were to actively address every reason that is now used as an excuse for international violence, such as rampant poverty, hunger, and homelessness around the world, the fundamental reasons that terrorists cite for their so-called "holy" wars would disappear, and they'd be exposed for the petty bullies they actually are.

Still, these changes won't happen overnight. It would mean taking a proactive stance on all fronts, instead of just trying to "put out fires," as is done in the current system. It would mean identifying and eliminating the cause of all those sociological "fires" that plague us now. It could take generations of hard work to move us from the violent mess we're mired in now to a state of true peace. But reaching that goal is certainly worth the effort!

In the world I imagine, society would function so well that many of the costs of living in the current system would be history, a point I'll discuss in more detail in the section on the price of poverty in the final chapter in this book on Poverty and Politics. For now, just switching from the chaotic industry that denies medical care to millions of people to a system that delivers all necessary health, dental, and vision services to every single individual would be a giant step forward for our country--and a major improvement in the lives of millions of Americans!

Chapter 10

True Justice

THE PRICE OF JUSTICE

I f you've read some of the earlier chapters in this book, you're familiar with my vision of a world where both learning and community service are lifelong habits, everyone is fully employed according to their training and abilities, and no one is forced to exist in a state of poverty.

Indeed, if these developments were to come about, shouldn't we assume that most of the problems we now experience with crime and violence would be a thing of the past?

Perhaps, but it's likely that some people would still commit crimes. After all, there are more things in the human heart, soul, and nervous system that could not be mended simply by removing most of the social stresses that plague the world today!

You see, I'm not talking about paradise. We humans don't have that power. I'm just thinking about the possibilities of a society in which problems are approached with more effective solutions than those that have been employed to date.

Even the most diehard law-and-order fanatic must agree that we could do much better than the system we have now, where criminals from the lower classes are often punished harshly for the smallest infractions, and many go on to commit more serious crimes than those actions that put them behind bars in the first place. And no one can deny that there's something seriously wrong when the richer the criminals and the more profit they reap from their wrongdoing, the greater the chance that they'll serve a short time, if at all, and do little or nothing to help their victims recoup their losses.

The challenge, then, is to develop a justice system in which all criminals repay both society and their victims according to the same scale, and rather than becoming more hardened in prison, they all serve sentences by serving their neighbors--and especially their victims.

My ideas on the subject can be encapsulated into one guiding principle: Justice builds security, while revenge destroys peace and is more expensive than the crime itself. This rule applies on both a personal and a societal level.

In the current system, wrongdoers serve sentences dictated by a complex system of often conflicting criminal codes. Rarely are they expected to make restitution to their victims, even though these people are always damaged financially and psychologically, and often physically. The effects are usually passed on to the rest of us in the form of higher costs for medical care, insurance, and welfare benefits. Then there are the costs of investigations, prosecutions, and the growing number of prisons designed to punish--to exact revenge from the criminals instead of reforming them--which do little more than give the rest of us a false sense of security.

How much better it would be if criminals paid for the damage they actually cause--and more. Thus, the cornerstone of my plan for improving the criminal justice system would be an inviolable rule that every lawbreaker would repay both society and their victims at least twice the amount of all costs incurred as a result of their crimes.

That amount would include the cost of all medical care, lost wages, and other crime-related expenses to the victims, as determined by the courts. Then there would be all the administrative costs as detailed above. Doubling those costs would apply only to a first offender. Repeat offenders would have to pay costs in ever-increasing multiples, up to a reasonable limit of five times the costs for subsequent offenses--until offenders smartened up and straightened out their act!

Obviously, the extent of such a "fine" would put a serious criminal into a deep hole for a very long time. In fact, some would be working off their legal debts for much of their lives. Well, that's the idea!

Besides the fact that the costs of crimes would be paid by the people who generate them, the legal system would have the right to oversee the activities of lawbreakers during all the time it takes them to repay their debts to their victims and society. This would be done not only to ensure that they repay their legal debts, but to minimize the chances that they'll break the law again.

Like so many of the other facets of society covered in this book, my ideas for overhauling the criminal justice system are much more complicated than the few details I've introduced here. In the next section on justice and responsibility, I'll discuss the subject in more depth.

As always, it's important to remember that the goal is to try to find ways to build a society in which the lowest-paid full-time worker on the planet is able to earn at least twice as much as it would cost to purchase all the basic goods and services necessary for a dignified existence. Only then will we be able to establish a truly democratic and peaceful society, for the first time in history.

JUSTICE AND RESPONSIBILITY

In the previous section on the price of justice, I explained my dream of a justice system in which all lawbreakers are required to pay "fines" that equal at least twice the total financial cost of their crimes, to both society and their victims. The key to this plan is something that is missing from the current justice system. In fact, it is almost non-existent throughout our present-day society: accepting total responsibility for one's own actions, especially for hurtful deeds.

My plan for criminals to repay their victims is nothing like the current system in which some criminals contribute to a general fund that is distributed to some crime victims to make up for a small part of the effects of crime on those victims. In the world I imagine, each person who commits any sort of crime would be required to make payments directly to the person or persons whom they have harmed, unless those people choose to have all or part of the money directed to an alternate beneficiary. A victim could also choose to receive their payments in person or through an intermediary.

The nature of prisons and who would spend time in them in the world I imagine would also be quite different from the present system. Currently, inmates who've committed all manner of crimes perform menial labor for pennies an hour; few have the opportunity to further their educations; younger inmates are locked up with older and more violent felons who abuse the weaker ones physically and sexually; and upon their release from prison, the majority return to a life of crime, usually to commit worse crimes than those that put them behind bars in the first place.

Thus, people locked away in today's concrete-and-steel prisons are denied the means to earn the money it would take to pay the kind of restitution I'm talking about. That's why I propose that we implement a plan to tap the valuable human resources that are being wasted in the current system.

In the world I imagine, only people who commit violent crimes would have to spend time behind bars. All other lawbreakers would serve their sentences by working in their communities while they are electronically monitored 24 hours a day.

As an avid fan of police-procedural TV shows, I'm aware that there can be problems in monitoring parolees. In an episode of one of the several "Law and Order" series, for instance, a felon managed to elude detection by transferring his ankle device onto his cat! To counter that possibility, I'm proposing a bit of science fiction that I predict will become fact very soon: One day probationers will wear devices that send the correct signal only when they're attached to the person whose DNA or other characteristics match their programs. Let's see them try to put that bracelet on a pet!

In the world I imagine, nonviolent criminals would be able to earn as much money as their skills allow. Like everyone else in the world, their basic expenses would be covered by their basic wages, but almost all their general wages--after their general taxes and personal investments are covered, as explained in the general tax payments

107

section of the chapter on Paying for Human Needs--would be directed toward paying off their legal fines. What's more, no one would get a discount for good behavior. Every criminal would be required to pay the full amount, and their probation would last until every penny of their fine is paid!

On the other hand, I'm not writing off the earning capacity of the people who would be locked up. I've already introduced two factors in the world I imagine that would make my plan cheaper than the current system: The reduction of social stresses would lead to lower crime rates, and incarceration would be limited to the small percentage of criminals who use or threaten violence in the commission of their crimes.

Giving prisoners the means to earn enough money to pay their legal fines, while contributing to instead of taking from society, means the social impact of crime in the world I imagine would be far less than it is with the penal system in place now. Add continually developing technology to the mix, and it's easy to imagine even imprisoned felons participating in more productive enterprises than they are allowed to do now.

The biggest problem would be security, which I discuss in greater depth in the next section on feeling secure. Then in the following section on ultimate crimes, I explain my plan for imposing fines on those who cause the deaths of other people, whether deliberate or accidental.

Meanwhile, it's important to remember that making sure criminals accept full responsibility for their actions, while ensuring that victims aren't financially damaged, will go a long way toward building and maintaining a society in which the lowest-paid full-time worker on the planet is able to earn at least twice as much as it costs to purchase all the basic goods and services necessary for a dignified existence.

All these elements would be needed if people are ever going to establish a truly democratic and peaceful society, for the first time in history.

FEELING SECURE

In the earlier section in this chapter on the price of justice, I introduced the idea that in the world I imagine, all criminals would pay at least twice the actual cost of their crimes both to society and their victims. Since everyone would receive a good education, be assured of well-paying and productive employment, and have all the basic goods and services they need, it's logical to assume that if my plan were fully implemented, few people would even think of committing a crime in the first place, much less make a habit of it.

With lower crime rates and guaranteed victim compensation, people would generally feel more secure than we do today, even though in my plan, people who commit nonviolent crimes would serve their sentences on the "outside," within their communities. But what about all those people who would be locked away from society because they employed violence in the commission of their crimes?

In the world I imagine, "lockups" would bear little resemblance to the concrete-and-steel boxes that are the standard in today's penal system. In my plan, the purpose of prison would not be so much to punish offenders but to teach, to rehabilitate, and especially to protect other people on the "outside" from those who don't control their baser impulses.

It's important to define the types of crime that, in my plan, would land a perpetrator in jail. Obviously, all those who use or threaten to use weapons or physical force, along with all those who rape or otherwise abuse anyone, no matter their relationship to their victims, would go to prison. Anyone convicted of drunk driving, which can result in a car crash, would serve jail time, and animal abuse would also merit mandatory jail time.

On the other hand, there are many laws that now generate jail time, such as the currently unbalanced drug laws, that need to be changed. For now, I'll say that in the world I imagine, users of any sort of illegal drug would not go to jail unless they used violence in the commission of a crime, or they at least drove under the influence. On the other hand, those who sell or distribute any drug without a license would earn time behind bars for a simple reason: Any drug can damage people who use it indiscriminately. Distributors must have the proper training to advise clients in the proper use of their products.

In my plan, life behind bars would not be what it is now. Forcing inmates into a demeaning atmosphere only reinforces the negative attitudes that got them into that situation in the first place. Instead, incarceration would be similar to a reasonably controlled military lifestyle in a self-contained community whose members would provide all the support systems that are part of running any small town on the outside. This would be done mostly by the inmates themselves, with just those professionals needed to round out security and other necessary services the inmates aren't qualified to manage.

Just like those serving their sentences on the outside, inmates would hold regular jobs, according to their level of training and skills, and be paid according to the same scale as everyone else doing that sort of work. And like the probationers serving sentences on the outside, those in prison would direct most of their general income toward their fines, and they'd stay in jail until that obligation was paid in full--no early release or time off for good behavior!

One caveat: These days, convicts do a lot of contract work for companies that handle secure data, such as taking mail orders by phone, a situation which gives criminals direct access to customers' credit-card and bank-account numbers. The problem with this arrangement is obvious, but it is still being done.

In the world I imagine, no one serving time for a crime, whether in prison or on probation, could work in any capacity that gives them access to data that they could use to commit more crimes. It's just common sense. Too many jobs currently go undone--such as upgrading abandoned buildings so everyone could have a place to live--to waste valuable human resources in a way that is bound to end up "biting" innocent people in the proverbial "rear end"!

In the world I imagine, prisons would be self-supporting communities, so inmates would ply almost every sort of trade that is needed to run any successful community. That way, they'd also be well prepared to fill similar productive roles when they return to the outside world.

The United States now spends more money than ever on prisons that return nothing for the investment. Obviously, something must be done to turn things around. Making all criminals take complete personal responsibility for their actions would go a long way toward establishing a society in which the lowest-paid full-time worker on the planet would be able to earn at least twice as much as it would cost to purchase all the basic goods and services necessary for a dignified existence.

We need to make these changes if we're ever going to establish a truly democratic and peaceful society, for the first time in history.

ULTIMATE CRIMES

In previous sections on what justice would be like in the world I imagine, I discussed ways in which people who commit crimes could work to repay both society and their victims for the damage they've done, even as they learn to be productive citizens of a truly just and democratic society. But even in the world I imagine, one thing can never be reversed: that is, any act, whether deliberate or accidental, that leads to the permanent disfigurement or death of another human being.

Obviously, fixing money damages in such cases is difficult. Many people feel the only adequate repayment for murder is for the person who took that life to give up his own. The issue is so intense in the current political environment that death-penalty advocates accuse those who oppose it of being too emotional and lacking objectivity.

On the other hand, enlightened societies understand that "an eye for an eye" is a relic of a primitive time when the value of most human life was measured in the services they provided for their "owners," who were always male and often related by blood or marriage. Moreover, the cost of executing criminals in the United States--including investigations, appeals, and years of incarceration on death row--is much higher than simply holding them in prison for the rest of their lives.

Then there are the cases of innocent people sentenced to die; those in which perpetrators have limited impulse control because of untreated, and often untreatable, medical conditions; and, finally, the governments that execute the members of minority groups at a higher rate than they do other criminals.

If we consider each argument in the death-penalty issue, then the choice of preserving perpetrators' lives in order to extract some practical social benefit tips the scales against execution based solely on revenge--which is, after all, the most negative and destructive emotion that humans experience!

How much better it would be if people were made to atone for their actions, whether deliberate or accidental, that lead to disability or death. Obviously, differences in intent would determine whether they also go to jail or remain free while they work to pay their fines.

The first rule would be that any intent to harm would condemn perpetrators to prison, and the measure of that intent would affect the length of time they stayed there and the size of the fines they would pay. Deliberate intent to kill would earn automatic life sentences for the killers, no matter the station of the victims or the circumstances of their deaths. Thus, people who hire others to kill would be just as culpable as those they hire, which isn't always the case today.

Then there are people who take chances which can lead to injury or death, such as drunken driving. In my plan, the sentence for a first drunk-driving offense would be mandatory jail time and alcoholism treatment; a fine of twice the amount of all administrative costs; and the loss of all non-work related driving privileges for a full year after their jail term is completed. In addition, they'd be subject to frequent unscheduled breath-analyzer tests to ensure that they don't drink at all during that time. And drunk drivers who cause injury or death would receive more jail time and higher fines, which brings me back to the issue of restitution.

With my plan, people who cause disfigurement of others would pay victims at least twice the value of their loss. In the event of death, they'd pay victims' families at least twice the value of lost wages and such services as household labor and psychological support. Of course, a victim's level of responsibility in an incident that leads to injury or death would affect any fines imposed on others who might also be involved. For instance, if the joint actions of two people leads to the death of one of them, the survivor would pay half of what he would have paid if he alone had caused the death and the other person was an unwitting victim.

Since the loss of a life is permanent, people who are responsible for another person's death would pay victims' families for the rest of their own lives. In the event of permanent injury, they'd pay the costs to victims during their victims' lifetimes. If their victims died prematurely as a result of the injury, the perpetrators would pay for the rest of their own lives, just as they'd have to if they'd caused an immediate death. As with other judicial cases, the people who cause harm to others would work in their communities or behind bars for money to pay fines, depending on the extent of their intent when they caused the damage.

Making people responsible for their actions, especially those that cause harm to others, would go a long way toward establishing a society in which the lowest-paid full-time worker on the planet is able to earn at least twice as much as it would cost to purchase all the basic goods and services necessary for a dignified existence. We need to make these changes if we're ever going to establish a truly democratic and peaceful society, for the first time in history.

MAKING JUST LAWS

As I began writing this section, first for my column in the *Arizona City Independent Edition*, I heard that a North

Carolina man was finally leaving prison after 35 years for stealing a black-and-white TV set. Since he was originally sentenced to life in prison, I guess he got off easy!

And I still can't figure out how Martha Stewart's languishing in jail for insider trading and lying to a grand jury made the world a better place. I don't understand why she couldn't just perform community service after she'd paid her fines!

Then there's the massive energy bill that Congress passed, supposedly to reduce the country's dependence on foreign oil. The joke at the time was, "No lobbyist left behind!"

Obviously, the consistent factor in these reports is that laws are inconsistent and often unfair, both to the public and to many individuals who find themselves crosswise of authority. That's why, as with other areas of social order, the only way to end poverty so we can establish peace in the world is to completely revamp our approach to the law, not only in the United States but all around the world.

As I've explained throughout this book, reforming society requires a comprehensive definition of basic human needs and an efficient means to deliver all necessary goods and services to each person on the planet at a cost of no more than half the amount that the lowest-paid full-time worker earns. We also need to clearly define every civil right that is inherent to every human being and make certain no laws anywhere conflict with these rights.

In the previous sections of this chapter, I suggested that wrongdoers should pay both society and their victims at least twice the cost of the damage they've done, and that people who use violence in the commission of their crimes should spend time behind bars as part of their sentences. I've also introduced the fact that without poverty, most conflicts, not only between nations but also between

115

individuals, would be diminished or even disappear.

Still, conflicts are bound to occur when laws and their application deny the rights of people based on gender, age, skin color, economic class, physical or mental disabilities, or other superficial and irrelevant factors. However, putting an end to poverty would no doubt improve the tendency of people and organizations to respect every individual's civil rights, no matter their station.

That is why in the world I imagine, no law would conflict with the inherent rights of any person or group, and no law could be enacted that benefits any person or organization to the detriment of any other individual or group of people.

In the administrating upward section of the chapter on Administering a Peaceful Planet, I described my plan in which every government employee would have to work their way up the ladder, beginning with service in local communities, and each elected office would be filled by a committee made up of people representing the community at large. No person would have more power than any other, and professionals could not move directly from a position in business, where profit is the primary motive, into any but the lowest level of government service, the community level. That means no one would be able to move directly into influential areas of the public sector and imperil the rights of any citizens because they insist on imposing the profit-first mentality that they exercised in the private sector.

In the sections on "paying" politics and a clean campaign in the chapter on Political Campaigns and Elections, I detailed the way in which money would no longer be the primary tool for gaining office. Thus, business would lose much of its power over lawmakers. In the most radical departure from the current government model, in the world I imagine, laws would no longer be voted on by elected representatives but by all citizens. And compromise would no longer be used in the legislative process, where powerful people gain even more from laws brimming with "pork" just so people in need can get a few measly "beans."

In my plan, any person or organization could propose a law, and the final wording of the bill would be worked out between the proponent of that law and members of the appropriate legislative committee. Each law would be written as simply as possible, with details broken down into individual bills whenever possible. In addition, no one could attach an unrelated rider to any legislative bill. Thus, no person or group would be able to extract any privilege for the favor of granting benefit where it should be applied anyway.

Once a law has been written, it would be published and discussed in the Political Action Newspaper and read and discussed on PAN radio and TV networks, all of which are described in the section on "paying" politics. Thus, every citizen would have ample opportunity to study and consider the pros and cons of every law that they'll be able to vote on at regular intervals.

That opportunity for citizens to vote on every law would mean that governments would, for the first time in history, be changed from representative republics into true democracies. Of course, some citizens do vote on some laws now, but there are currently limits to which laws are open to a public vote and which citizens can actually vote on them, because of a lack of education or station or other superficial limitations.

In the world I imagine, with educational opportunities available to all and easy access to complete and accurate political information, every citizen would have all the tools they need to fully participate in this most basic exercise of democracy. With full participation, citizens would enjoy an effective voice in government, and the result would be a lessening of conflict around the world.

Chapter 11

Respecting Civil Rights

A QUESTION OF VALUES

As I was working on the essays for this book, I was
acutely aware that some people don't understand
certain points I make because of a problem that exists when
people try to discuss such topics as politics, religion, etc.
Everyone has different experiences in their lives, and the
values they espouse differ based on those experiences.

Among the many factors that contribute to an
individual's values are family dynamics, religious training,
education, social relationships, and work experiences.
Throughout a lifetime, a person will come into contact with
many different influences, all of which become part of the
complex puzzle that makes up that individual's psyche.

For example, a person might learn from their family of
origin to distrust people who are of a different color or
nationality than they, yet their religious training might be
based on the principle that we must all love one another,

including those who are different from us. The lesson that prevails depends upon other factors in their life experience. Thus, someone who is raised to think of certain people as less than human might, over the years, learn lessons that help them overcome their early training of hatred and lead them to perform positive services for people they might, at one time, have considered their enemies.

I approach social issues from the perspective of a belief that all humans are deserving of respect, that everyone deserves to enjoy life with dignity, and that poverty is the antithesis of that sort of existence. Indeed, Mohandas K. (Mahatma) Gandhi said, "Poverty is the worst form of violence."

In my writing, I often focus on various institutions and policies that promote the status quo, which depends upon a perpetual class of people who live in poverty, and suggest innovative solutions to problems so that humans might one day bring an end to poverty everywhere and finally establish peace throughout the planet, for the first time in history.

Still, the opinions and reactions that some people have toward my ideas depend upon the range of their experiences and their attitudes regarding the subjects under discussion. Some people might want to preserve institutions that currently serve them well, even if those same agencies don't serve the needs of all people the way they should.

For example, school programs that work very well for many students fail to meet the needs of too many others. People who do well in school probably don't want changes made to the current system, fearing they would be hurt by those changes. Since I propose giving every student control over an individual learning program, among other things, my ideas would have no effect on those people who now benefit from the status quo. At the same time, they would offer real help to those students who are currently neglected by a rigid bureaucracy that depends more on mass test results than on real teaching programs designed for individuals.

But the concept of providing adequate education for every person might not matter to someone who doesn't care about people whose needs are not being met by the current system. That's why discussing the issues covered in this book requires that all parties agree that human dignity is a God-given--or for those who prefer the non-religious reference, nature-ordained--right that is universal to all human beings.

And what of people who don't believe in this principle of human rights? For instance, certain government authorities have made the stunning assertion that the Bill of Rights in the United States Constitution applies only to American citizens and that the principles outlined in the Geneva Convention do not apply to everyone who engages in combat.

It is important to remember that the framers of the Constitution did not apply the principles of freedom to women, slaves, Native Americans, or other people of color, yet time and history have brought some enlightenment to a great many people, though not all, in that regard. Thus, one can hope that similar lessons will occur respecting the currently erroneous administrative policies that limit the rights of so many people.

In fact, those two documents, along with a few others composed in the last century, list ways in which every human being should be treated. They are merely the earliest steps that humans have taken in a universal journey to identify and establish the right of every human being to respectful treatment, no matter where they were born, where they live, or how they act in times of war and other conditions of stress.

If all people ever do is return blow for blow, the human struggle will never end. Only when we offer a chance for everyone to live a life of dignity and self-respect by ending poverty altogether will humans be able to end the practice of war on this planet. And that will only happen when each person is able to purchase all the basic goods and services necessary for a dignified existence at a cost of no more than half the amount earned by the lowest-paid full-time worker on the planet.

Only then will we be able to build a truly peaceful society around the world, for the first time in history.

CIVIL RIGHTS FOR ALL

My dictionary defines "civil rights" as "the rights, privileges, and protection given to *citizens*" (Oxford American Dictionary, pocket edition, 1979/1980). The book goes on to explain that the "civil rights movement" is "an organized movement to secure civil rights for blacks *and other minorities* in the U.S." (The italics in both definitions are mine!)

Many civil-rights activists need to check their dictionaries--and their hearts--so they can get their perspective straight on the issue of just who all those civil rights belong to. They seem to believe that only members of their minority group own the power to define which rights apply to members of other minority groups. Besides denying many rights to gays and lesbians, people involved in civil-rights movements have actually informed me, a person disabled by chronic illness, that people with disabilities have no civil rights--the Americans with Disabilities Act notwithstanding!

Sadly, this attitude is neither unusual nor new. The history of civil rights has always involved groups that fought to obtain their own rights, then denied those rights to others. Each November Americans gather around sumptuous turkey dinners to commemorate a group of religious pilgrims who left their European homeland to establish a colony where they were free to worship as they chose. Unfortunately, those same pilgrims adamantly refused to extend that right to others.

In fact, the Puritans of Massachusetts are probably best known for the witch trials of Salem, in which 19 people were executed and scores of others tortured and imprisoned when the false claims of two young girls incited the prejudices of that fanatical religious sect. And though the colony would have failed without aid from local natives, within a few years these immigrants were waging war on the same Indians with whom they'd celebrated their first "harvest festival" in 1621.

After America gained independence as a nation, abolitionists began fighting to free black slaves. On the other hand, most of the men and some of the women working for that cause refused to extend the same consideration to women, though the experience of most women paralleled that of many slaves and the earliest suffragists were also abolitionists. Thus, when the 15th Amendment was ratified, the law applied only to black men. It was another 50 years before women of any color gained the legal right to vote in national elections.

That's why I'm not surprised that many people working for the betterment of people of color don't understand that civil rights are inherent to every human being. Moreover, this narrow attitude is not limited to our own country.

Regarding the Third Reich, Martin Niemoeller explained, "In Germany, they came first for the

Communists, and I didn't speak up because I wasn't a Communist. Then they came for the Jews, and I didn't speak up because I wasn't a Jew. Then they came for the trade unionists, and I didn't speak up because I wasn't a trade unionist. Then they came for the Catholics, and I didn't speak up because I was a Protestant. Then they came for me, and by that time no one was left to speak up."

Though he acknowledged several different groups whose rights--and even lives--were abridged by that infamous regime, even Pastor Niemoeller ignores the minority group that Hitler's minions targeted first. Niemoeller's statement should have opened with this sentence: "In Germany, they came first for the people with physical, mental, and emotional disabilities, and I didn't speak up because I was healthy."

The sad fact is, many execution methods that were later used to murder millions of people in Nazi death camps were originally "tested" on small groups of people with various disabilities and physical abnormalities, such as dwarfism. Others with serious and even incurable medical conditions spent the war years in government "hospitals," where doctors performed cruel medical experiments that enhanced their suffering and often led to their early demise.

Those who claim that certain civil rights are the exclusive purview of their particular group and apply only to those who share a similar experience should remember the lessons of Nazi Germany. History is replete with examples of groups that were targeted, harassed, tortured, and eventually wiped out because others lacked the courage or concern to speak up for the rights of everyone.

In the world I imagine, society will protect all the inherent rights of every single human being, no matter their minority status. This can be accomplished only by eliminating the tool that people in power now use to perpetuate the conflicts between minority groups: poverty.

By limiting access to the resources that people need to enjoy a dignified existence, governments and businesses are able to exercise more control over the lives of the people in their sphere of influence. People and groups who are being manipulated in this way often view other individuals and groups who need the same resources in a competitive light, and vice-versa.

These people usually fail to understand that if people were to cooperate, and even join forces, with those they perceive as their enemies, they might be able to generate enough power to upset the status quo and spread the resources around for all to enjoy. Thus, poor people who fight among themselves for mere crumbs could become a mighty army for good and, with positive force, convince the government to help them work to end poverty forever.

Of course, poverty will end only when all the basic goods and services necessary for a dignified existence are available to every person on the planet at a cost of no more than half the amount earned by the lowest-paid full-time worker. When that becomes a reality, humans can finally begin to build a peaceful society where no one questions the rights of any other person, for the first time in the history of this planet.

CIVIL RIGHTS AND LABOR

In the previous section on civil rights for all, I explained that no single person or group, whether they're in the majority or belong to a minority group, can limit the basic rights that are inherent to every single human being. In the current political environment, this is a volatile issue. However, it is absolutely necessary for society, if it is to be successful, to identify all the rights that belong to each human being before we can begin to solve the problem of poverty and build a peaceful society.

Some rights are so basic that they should seem obvious, such as every person's right to earn enough money to pay for basic food, housing, medical care, etc. Unfortunately, it almost seems to be an inherent part of the social design that a shocking number of people are denied access to these basic resources.

Throughout the world, billions of people are unable to earn enough money to purchase many, if not most, of the goods and services they need to enjoy a dignified existence, even when they spend most of their waking hours at some kind of labor. Worse, many people aren't even allowed to do any work at all in order to earn enough money to purchase what they really need.

In the United States, for instance, the amount of money paid to millions of people on welfare or disability programs ensures that they live far below the poverty line, but if they try to earn money to make up the difference, they will be denied access to part or all of their government benefits. Then they're usually left to perform labor that pays little and offers no medical and other benefits--if they can even find a job or, in the case of people with many types of disability, if they're capable of doing any substantial work at all.

The policy of forcing people with few resources to choose between meager social support and the little money they can earn--while being threatened with receiving nothing at all if they make a wrong move--puts me in mind of Pharaoh's decree that the Hebrew slaves be forced to make bricks without straw (Exodus chapter 5). This policy leaves the most vulnerable people in society caught between their need for help to survive and the right of every person to be a productive member of society.

The solution is exactly what I've defined throughout this book as the goal of any successful society: Each person should be able to purchase all the basic goods and services necessary for a dignified existence at a cost of no more than half the amount earned by the lowest-paid full-time worker on the planet. This means everyone must be allowed to perform work that pays at least twice the amount needed to purchase those basic goods and services, according to their individual capacity to do so.

For instance, every disabled person must be allowed to perform the best-paid work that they're qualified to do within the limits of their disability. At the same time, they should receive all the basic goods, social services, and especially the medical care they need, in exchange for a percentage of the regular cost paid by a healthy full-time worker, on a sliding scale corresponding to their degree of disability. This assurance that they will not be forced to live in poverty because of their disability will have a positive effect, not only on their mental and emotional outlook, but also on their physical condition.

The fact that disabled people would be not only allowed but encouraged to engage in productive activity within the scope of their physical and mental abilities, for their own benefit and that of society, would also contribute to their improved outlook and condition. What's more, allowing disabled people to engage in whatever work they can perform in exchange for having all their basic needs completely met would have a long-term beneficial effect on the social "bottom line."

A similar combination of employment and public support would help single mothers and others with limited education and training to raise themselves and their families out of poverty. It would be much cheaper in the long run to use money now paid out as welfare benefits over many years to train people for better-paying jobs while providing safe child-care services close to a parent's home, job and/or school, plus all the basic goods and services the family needs until the parent can learn enough to join the work force on a full-time basis.

In fact, many who struggle in despair on welfare could be trained as child-care providers, and some could even open day-care centers with a little help from the same agencies that now pay them not to work. The social benefit would not only be an immediate improvement in the lives of these women and their children, it would enhance their children's hopes for the future and that of so many others too.

While these solutions might seem logical, many people don't like to think of people who are poor and/or disabled as having the same rights, feelings, and needs as "the rest of us." That's a big part of the reason that people in minority groups are often stymied by bureaucratic red tape, such as the aforementioned labor restrictions that now apply to disabled people and poor single mothers. How much better and more profitable for society would it be to do the right thing in the first place, with none of the restrictive red tape that only hinders progress for individuals and for society as a whole?

Yet, even if governments do take steps to end poverty by providing all the basic goods and services necessary for a dignified existence at a price that everyone can afford, we would still have to ensure that no person's civil rights in any area are abridged or denied. Otherwise, we cannot build a truly peaceful society. Since that aspect of civil rights is far more complicated, in the next section of this chapter I'll discuss some of the more sensitive types of civil rights that must be guaranteed for every single person, especially those that seem to conflict with each other.

CONFLICTING CIVIL RIGHTS

As I explained in the last two sections of this chapter, civil rights are inherent to and must be guaranteed for every human being. But even as we strive to build an equitable society, many of these rights continue to be debated. As I discussed in the previous section on civil rights and labor, simply acknowledging the right of every person not to exist in a state of poverty isn't enough; supporting the right to earn enough to pay for all necessary basic goods and services is also a vital factor in assuring and maintaining the dignity of every individual. Thus, we must acknowledge and respect those civil rights that bear no relation to whether a person exists in a state of poverty or not.

For example, one area of contention is the right of people not to be exposed to second-hand smoke. Of course, a smoke-free environment is one aspect of our basic right to live in a healthy environment. This means that smokers must balance their responsibility toward the rest of us with their right to puff. A third party in the issue, the tobacco industry, cannot claim any of the rights that belong to either of the other two parties, but they do have a responsibility to be part of any solution.

There are two major tobacco issues, the industry's responsibility toward people who've been damaged by their products and the right of non-smokers not to be exposed to smoke. The second is the easiest to manage, but that's rarely being done in equitable fashion. For instance, most cities are banning smoking from public places, including all restaurants and bars.

As an ex-smoker who gave up the "filthy weed" in 1969, I understand smokers' desire for a tobacco "fix." But since I'm now allergic to smoke, among many other things, I also have a right not to be assaulted by noxious fumes in public places. On the other hand, I agree that total smoking bans in all public places go too far.

Of course, in the world I imagine, nobody would smoke in the first place, but we live in the real world, so we need to find a solution that would consider everyone's rights and desires. In my opinion, a limited number of restaurants and bars in each community should be able to purchase smoking licenses. That way, money from expensive license fees would be directed toward health care and every city would have a small number of leisure establishments that cater to the puffer crowd. To avoid surprising those who choose to avoid smoke, these places must be clearly identified as smoking establishments in all advertising and with large signs posted on both sides of every entrance. Thus, everyone's rights would be totally respected.

A more complicated issue is the way money is spent to make up for the industry's decades-long practice of lying about tobacco addiction. While tobacco companies must now pay billions of dollars to states, a huge share of this cash has gone directly into the pockets of plaintiffs' attorneys.

There's nothing wrong with someone earning an honest buck, but some attorneys' fees outweigh their contributions to the cause. I understand the risk and expenses that attorneys take on when they become involved in contingency cases, but reasonable legal limits must be set on the percentage any attorney can collect in any case, especially those with such massive settlements. Moreover, most of the money from tobacco companies should be directed toward two goals: paying directly for the medical needs of people suffering from tobacco-related illnesses, and discouraging non-smokers, especially young people, from taking up that filthy habit. Money from tobacco settlements should not be used for any other purpose.

On the other hand, no individual should be able to sue tobacco companies on their own. Information about the dangers of tobacco has been available for nearly half a century, and no one was ever forced to use it. Tobacco executives lied to everyone, so they shouldn't have to pay millions of dollars to a few people with the smartest lawyers, while everyone else receives nothing for the damage that smoking has done to them.

As I've discussed in the sections on rights and responsibilities, healthy medicine, and many others, it is absolutely necessary for individuals and corporations to do their part to help establish a more equitable society. Tobacco is just one area in which this balance is necessary. Other areas include the right of a person to own a weapon, balanced with care in handling the weapon. Manufacturing and using various chemical substances responsibly is another sensitive area, and there are many, many others where common sense and wisdom must be used more judiciously than they often are now.

Of course, society currently has almost no incentive to solve most of these problems in equitable fashion. Real change will come only when we realize that applying logic to problem solving is the least expensive approach to reaching the goal of a society in which each person is able to purchase all the basic goods and services necessary for a dignified existence at a cost of no more than half the amount earned by the lowest-paid full-time worker on the planet. So, even as we consider the minutiae of conflict resolution, we must remember the "big picture" and do everything possible to end poverty all over the world.

In the next section of this chapter, I discuss one of the most contentious areas of civil rights, freedom of religion. In this area, as in everything, we must strive to respect the rights and beliefs, or lack of belief, of everyone. That isn't always easy, but it is absolutely necessary if we are ever going to build a truly peaceful society, for the first time in history.

CIVIL RIGHTS AND RELIGION

When I first broached this subject in my column in the *Arizona City Independent Edition*, I'd recently learned that someone I knew was soon to wed his fiancée in their hometown. Because they reside in a European country, the couple first attended a civil ceremony before they could hold a religious wedding, if they chose to do so. Of course, they have the option to forgo the latter ritual, yet still enjoy all the benefits of their legal union.

This couple happens to be heterosexual, but the clear separation of church and state in most countries of Europe made it a simple matter for governments to reform their marriage laws when they decided to acknowledge the right of civil union for same-sex couples. On this side of the pond, however, the government not only licenses clergy members to act as civil agents in a legal ceremony, it allows the leaders of a small number of churches to dictate who can and who cannot enjoy the legal benefits of what is first a civil arrangement.

Of course, church leaders have a right to decide who they accept as members and who may engage in their ceremonies and sacraments. It's important to note that many churches accept everyone as members, so restrictions within certain churches impose little hardship on most people. However, no person or group has the right to impose rules on people who are not part of their organization, especially when those rules limit the civil rights of any member of society.

An obvious historic example of this abuse is the way religion was used to support slavery and segregation. These days, most people know better than to use religion to influence laws that discriminate on the basis of race, but racial divisions do continue in many churches today. Some might choose to handle the situation through confrontation, while others simply choose to attend another church.

Meanwhile, the religious beliefs of many people still conflict with the civil rights of women, children, and people with alternative gender orientation. It's important to note that while everyone has a right to a personal opinion, no one has the right to deny someone their right to work at whatever job they qualify for, to live wherever they choose, and to enjoy the entire range of benefits that belong to every human being.

Holding negative feelings toward someone is prejudice; acting them out is discrimination. Prejudice is between oneself and God; discrimination is a crime against society.

It is interesting to note that in recent years the United States government has spent an inordinate portion of its resources trying to prevent the establishment of a theocracy overseas, yet the same cannot be said for what the same people in power are trying to do in this country. If the United States wants to impose a wall between religion and government in places like Iraq and Afghanistan, then we must do the same here at home.

Lately there's been a legal question as to whether the Pledge of Allegiance should contain the words "under God." It is significant to note that two issues drove politicians to add those words in 1954: anticommunism and segregation. The current discussion generally ignores the 1943 decision in *West Virginia State Board of Education v. Barnette* when, even before the word "God" was added, the Supreme Court ruled that no one could be compelled to salute the flag or recite the Pledge of Allegiance *because it is a religious ceremony.* (Italics mine!)

Despite the law, the flag ceremony is generally recited in a time and place in which all students are required to be present, so it's easy to identify those who choose not to salute or recite the Pledge. Despite their legal right to dissent, this arrangement sets up children for ill treatment ranging from simple teasing to vicious physical abuse because of their beliefs. Sadly, many teachers not only encourage this mistreatment of the children they're supposed to protect, but some even torment those children who, for personal and/or religious reasons, choose not to join the others in an enforced display of nationalism.

This crime--and it is a completely illegal situation!-- could be prevented simply by requiring schools to hold the flag ceremony in an auditorium or other large area before students are required to be present. This would give those students who choose not to attend the ceremony a better chance of remaining anonymous--and safe!

In this discussion of religion and civil rights, it is important to note that though religion often wields an inordinate, and often inappropriate, amount of power in many areas, many people of religious faith have accomplished wonderful things because of their faith. While society must rein in the negative influence of religious organizations, we must encourage the positive contributions, especially by people who are trying to end poverty and establish peace.

With their help, we might one day be able to build a society in which each person receives all the basic goods and services necessary for a dignified existence at a cost of no more than half the amount earned by the lowest-paid full-time worker on the earth. With the help of people of religious faith, we might then be able to enjoy the future on a truly peaceful planet.

DISCRIMINATION VERSUS CULTURE

In the previous section on civil rights and religion, I mentioned the unfortunate role of religion in the history of racial segregation in the United States. On the other hand, we must remember that religious faith not only inspired the civil-rights movement, but many churches provided a rich source of workers for this vital cause.

Our country has made a lot of social progress in the last half century, but a great deal of work remains to be done before justice is guaranteed for every human being all over the planet. We must do everything we can to end discrimination based on race, national origin, religion, disability, gender orientation, marital and family status, and all other factors that people use as an excuse to set people and groups apart from the mainstream. Intelligence and creativity can also be triggers for discrimination--certainly a self-defeating policy for any society.

One way to support and protect the civil rights of all people is to avoid using negative words and statements that demean minority groups and their members. Of course, this doesn't mean avoiding all mention of a person's minority status. Too often the tendency to be "politically correct" has the effect of "ignoring the elephant in the room." But we must be sensitive about the way we react to the factors that make people different from each other.

A recent example of "political correctness" run amok

here in Arizona is the negative reaction that many people have had to language- and culture-specific DUI courts. The State of Arizona has been accused of racial segregation because many Hispanic and Native American offenders were assigned to programs which respect their language and customs.

The cultural courts were developed as a voluntary alternative because minority offenders generally don't fare as well as Anglo offenders in mainstream programs. It turns out that graduates of these cultural courts have a greater success rate than that of all offenders in English-only programs. Perhaps the regular courts could learn something from the cultural courts.

If members of minority groups are allowed to choose between functioning in the mainstream or within the language and culture with which they're most familiar, some will choose the mainstream and some will stay within their own culture. As long as the choice exists, and the alternative doesn't disempower anyone, then the policy can't be called "segregation." On the contrary, respecting a person's cultural autonomy is probably the most important reason for the success of minority-oriented programs in all areas of society.

On the other hand, Arizona has tried to force non-English speaking students to spend the entire school day in total English immersion programs. Total immersion for part of each day is a great way for someone to learn English, but all-day English immersion only means that even more Hispanic students will fall farther behind in their non-language classes, eventually dropping out of school at the highest rate of any group in the state.

In the world I imagine, any misguided policy maker who would dare impose such a draconion "integration" policy would be forced to spend a day--just one single day!--in a classroom in which everyone speaks a language they don't understand. At the end of the day, they would have to take a rigorous test on all the subjects that were covered in that foreign language. Then let's see how much non-language educational data they were able to pick up!

I agree that immigrants should learn the language of their adopted country, but imposing harsh rules upon an already powerless group is, at best, ineffective and--especially in the case of English-immersion educational programs--much too expensive in the long run. Whatever money schools save on bilingual teachers is more than outweighed by the future social costs of underemployment, unemployment, welfare, law enforcement, prison, etc., that will be the fate of so many students now being denied the comprehensive education that could help them become fully productive, tax-paying citizens of their adopted country.

As I began writing this section, first as an article for the *Arizona City Independent Edition*, thousands of immigrants were staging massive demonstrations in Phoenix, Los Angeles, and other cities around the country. In the next section in this chapter, I'll discuss how many of the ideas I've discussed throughout this book could resolve many of the conflicts related to immigration and outsourcing. In the section on colonialism and poverty in the final chapter on Poverty and Politics, I explain why illegal immigration is a natural result of a disastrous historic economic policy.

Of course, the primary goal should be to end poverty everywhere by making it possible for each person to purchase all the basic goods and services necessary for a dignified existence at a cost of no more than half the amount earned by the lowest-paid full-time worker on the planet. Only then will we be able to build a peaceful society in every corner of the world, for the first time in history.

IMMIGRATION AND MORE

I began writing this book first as a series of articles in which I could discuss creative ideas for ending poverty in every corner of the world. As I began this section, a couple of related issues exploded in the headlines--and in the streets of cities on two different continents.

In the United States, hundreds of thousands of people protested legislation that could turn undocumented workers into felons. At the same time, young people demonstrated in France against laws that would allow employers to fire them without explanation anytime within their first two years of employment. Add the touchy issue of companies laying off higher-paid Americans and replacing them with lower-wage foreign workers, outside the country and even in the United States, and it's obvious that the global employment situation has deteriorated steadily in recent years.

These problems are a result of government policies that perpetuate poverty by imposing a wide range of pay scales, benefits, and market costs for people in different regions, countries, and classes. The issues are complex and everyone involved has valid points to make; no one is entirely right or entirely wrong in these matters. But until governments address the underlying cause of the problems, the situation will only worsen.

Many immigrants risk everything to come to the United States, whether by legal means or otherwise, because they can't earn enough in their native countries to care for their families at home. On the other hand, undocumented aliens are often paid less than legal residents, which has a negative effect on wages and benefits for everyone.

Despite all the people desperate to get into this country, millions of native-born American citizens barely survive in a state of abject poverty. Even middle-class American workers who haven't experienced wage, benefit, or job losses are feeling the effects of stagnant income levels in the face of rising prices. Generally, only those at the highest income levels have enjoyed improved earning and purchasing power since the beginning of the 21st century.

Unfortunately, these problems are rarely improved by the often conflicting band-aid approaches taken by public and private agencies. Tighter border security will not ease wage competition within the country, and it certainly won't eliminate job competition with other countries, nor will it help anyone who is jobless or homeless, in or outside of the United States.

In the jobs, wages, and benefits section of the chapter on Universal Employment, I explained that if every country in the world accepted a universal standard of pay for similar jobs, no matter where or by whom those jobs are performed, then no one would be forced to travel to other countries just to earn enough money to care for their families. In the sections on delivering services and delivering goods in the chapter on Meeting Human Needs, I discussed the need for providing every person in the world with easy access to basic goods and services at standard rates in exchange for fair employment.

The chapters on Universal Education and Universal Health Care explained why everyone in the world must have full access to lifelong learning and adequate medical services according to individual need. And finally, the chapter on Universal Employment explained that providing full and fair employment to everyone is a necessary part of a holistic approach to ending poverty and establishing peace around the world.

I've also discussed the fact that the current system of governing from the top down will never solve the problems causing so much conflict around the world. On the contrary, that very system has generated, or at least aggravated, most of the problems, whether by deliberate action or by ignoring situations and/or groups with unmet needs, until they explode into often-violent confrontations. The solutions will come only when we establish a truly democratic government which respects the basic needs of every person on the planet.

If policies like those I've outlined throughout this book were implemented in every single corner of every country in the world, no one would be forced to leave their loved ones behind and risk deportation or death, just to scrounge for a job so they can earn enough money to do little more than feed their families.

The daily news always reminds me of the fact that so many problems could not only be improved, most could actually be solved, if poverty were eliminated everywhere. As I mention throughout this book, that will occur only when each person in the world has the means to purchase all the basic goods and services necessary for a dignified existence at a cost of no more than half the amount earned by the lowest-paid full-time worker on the planet. Only then will we be able to build a peaceful society around the world.

REMEMBER THE CHILDREN

Each year our national consciousness is directed to the celebration of parents. Institutions ranging from local churches to retail stores tell us to "Remember Mom" and "Don't Forget Dad."

No doubt many parents deserve respect for their sacrifices in raising children. But what of those children who are abused by their parents? What do victims owe to the people who torture them in so many ways?

Most people know Mothers Day is celebrated in May and Fathers Day in June. But did you know that April is National Child Abuse Prevention Month? I wasn't aware of it, though I'm an adult survivor of abuse.

My relatives' attempts to continue punishing me for my illness, after all the years I'd suffered their physical abuse and medical neglect, continued into my 50s. Though they're responsible for the extent of my disability, I fought them as I'd always done, by trying to talk sensibly to people who'll never accept me as a human being with basic civil rights. Until their attitude changes, I've had to accept that my first duty is to protect myself from their toxicity, which only exacerbates my medical condition. The choice is theirs.

One day I'll share my story, but for now, I want to introduce some basic facts about abuse. Perhaps I can help someone who needs to understand that if it's happening to them or to someone they love, they have a right to do what they must to make it stop.

Perhaps the biggest myth that prevents abuse victims from getting protection, especially from their own parents, is the claim that "parents give children life." Thus, all children are expected to respect their parents, even when parents so completely disrespect their own children.

My favorite response to this claim comes from Kahlil Gibran's *The Prophet* (Alfred A. Knopf, Inc., 1923, 1951), in his poem "On Children":

"They come through you but not from you,

"And though they are with you yet they belong not to you."

Though Gibran never uses the word in this poem, his vivid imagery credits the source of life as God:

"You are the bows from which your children as living arrows are sent forth.

"The archer sees the mark upon the path of the infinite, and He bends you with His might that His arrows may go swift and far."

Thus, it is not parents who give children life but the Creator. Children are a gift from God, and parents must treat them with tender loving care. Abusing a child is a rejection of that precious gift, an act of disrespect toward the Great Giver of Life.

Though the 20th chapter of Exodus, in verse 5, connects "iniquity of the fathers" to idol worship, I often wonder if the warning that "visiting the iniquity of the fathers on the children, on the third and the fourth generations of those who hate Me" (KJV) refers to the fact that the abuse of children--rejection of God's most sacred Gift to humans--tends to run in families, since parents who abuse children are likely to have been abused themselves.

On the other hand, abused children don't necessarily become abusers too. The behavior can be unlearned; the cycle can be broken. It is a matter of education and choice. But if we don't talk about it, it cannot be eradicated, and victims will never find a way out of the cycle of abuse.

It's important to note that no matter what form abuse takes, the goal is always the same: power. Abusers have an inordinate need to control someone who can't fight back. Abuse, whether verbal, physical, sexual, or medical, is merely the tool that the abuser uses to exercise control over someone they consider weak, which is the only way abusers can feel powerful about themselves.

Abusers become angry when victims speak out, but it is the only way to protect their victims and stop the abuse. That's why we must bring the issue into the light and teach children to stand up for themselves and speak out until they find someone to protect them. Children must understand that anyone can be an abuser: strangers, friends, and relatives--especially parents. Children must be taught that when they're betrayed by the people they should be able to trust more than anyone else, parents lose the right to their loyalty and respect.

In the world I imagine, poverty ("the worst violence," according to Mohandas K. (Mahatma) Gandhi) will be a distant memory and war will be a mere footnote in the history books. In such a society, abusive parents will be exposed and children will be protected from harm. Then, and only then, can we build a truly peaceful society throughout the world.

Chapter 12

Poverty and Politics

THE TROUBLE WITH POVERTY

I n the section on the feudalism of labor in the chapter on Universal Employment, I explained that the current employment model practiced in most parts of the world is based on customs perfected in the Middle Ages. In ancient days, all benefits derived from the landlord, whereas they now come from employers. When modern-day employees lose their jobs, the equivalent of being thrown off the landlord's estate in the old days, they lose any semblance of security that comes with a regular paycheck, including access to medical insurance--especially in the United States--vacation pay, and numerous other benefits.

A candid appraisal of economic tradition shows that policies still in place after thousands of years have always been detrimental to the welfare of most people. If you've read much of this book, you understand why I believe it is long past time to implement new social policies that would benefit everyone on the planet. Still, it's not easy to buck tradition, especially when so many of these policies appear to benefit the most powerful people in society: the wealthy.

On the other hand, if it were proven that policies that seem to benefit the rich actually cost people of privilege--indeed, all people--far more than anyone should have to pay, then more people might be willing to take a more organized approach toward the goal of ending poverty everywhere. But first, we must understand exactly what poverty is.

The Random House Dictionary of the English Language (1987, Second Edition, Unabridged) defines "poverty" as: "1. the state or condition of having little or no money, goods, or means of support; condition of being poor; indigence."

That seems easy enough to say, but it doesn't explain why so many people around the world are forced to spend their entire lives in that state of need. Perhaps the *Oxford American Dictionary* (1980, Pocket Edition) offers more insight into the issue by listing "inferiority" as its third definition for "poverty."

Indeed, poverty is not merely the lack of resources needed to enjoy a dignified existence; it is a general societal attitude toward people who live in poverty. This is because people at all levels of society, including many who are poor, believe that poverty somehow marks one as less deserving of respect--and therefore, social support--than people who have more money.

Throughout this book, I refer to many current policies that reflect this attitude, so I won't go into them here. Suffice to say that any policy that hinders steady progress toward ending poverty everywhere should be replaced with one or more that helps move humanity toward that goal.

Still, one wonders who benefits from the perpetuation

of poverty. Why does it exist in the first place, and why does society force anyone to continue to suffer this pitiful condition? The answers to those questions are deeply rooted in human history. They are a direct result of the exercise of power of one person or group of people over another person or group. But rather than rehashing events of the past that cannot be changed, it is time to set aside the negative practices and start building a positive society, with no more poverty or conflict between people and nations.

That will only happen when we begin to understand how and why the practice of concentrating most of the world's wealth in the hands of a small minority, while denying so many even the necessities of life, hurts everyone, including those people who now enjoy the illusion of power that comes with having more money than they can ever use. In the next section on the price of poverty, I'll discuss the negative effects that poverty has on everyone, including members of the middle and upper classes.

Until then, it is vital that we remember that the time has come for humans to focus our collective energies toward building a system in which the lowest-paid full-time worker on the planet has the means to earn at least twice as much as it costs to purchase all the basic goods and services necessary to enjoy a dignified existence. This must include all the training and education that each person needs to perform the type of labor for which they are best suited, so they can be part of the effort to organize and run a truly well-functioning society.

Only then will poverty finally be relegated to the history books. Only then can we begin to establish a peaceful society throughout the world, for the first time in history.

THE PRICE OF POVERTY

In the previous section on the trouble with poverty, I explained that one factor that perpetuates that depressing condition is a belief in the inferiority of poor people. However, that concept is belied by the number of poor people who accomplish great things, especially in service to their fellow human beings.

A recent CNN report reminded me of the many parents of murdered children who focus their energies toward improving conditions in their poor neighborhoods. For instance, after Queen Brown's son was shot last year, the host of WTPS-AM 1080's "What's Going On?" discusses violence-related issues on her Miami radio talk show.

Other people born into poverty use their unique talents and skills to amass impressive fortunes, then dedicate large portions of their wealth to help poor people. As a baseball fan, I enjoy the fact that Sammy Sosa learned the game by hitting makeshift balls with sticks and fielding with used milk cartons. He now devotes large portions of his considerable income to businesses and social projects that provide jobs and services to help poor people in his hometown of San Pedro de Macoris, Dominican Republic. One of those projects is a sports academy where talented young athletes learn to play with the best equipment available.

On the other hand, the tabloids are full of reports of self-indulgent rich people, such as the heiress whose recent DUI led her into a legal quagmire. After driving on a suspended license and appearing late for court dates, she was sentenced to jail for repeatedly breaking the rules of her extremely lenient probation. So, money does not signify class in its truest sense.

Obviously, poor people pay the highest price for this

awful condition. Some costs are financial, such as higher prices at inner-city supermarkets--if any of those are left. A recent study showed that most inner-city neighborhoods don't even have grocery stores anymore! Another cost is the amount of time poor people waste dealing with red tape just to obtain such necessities as food, housing, and medical care.

Then there's the cost to those who try to help poor people with efforts that are, at best, patchy. Burnout among people frustrated by pointless regulations and endless hard-luck stories is not only expensive, it can have negative effects on the compassion that leads people into a life of service in the first place.

There are also costs that affect a powerful ruling class that tries to keep a tight rein on the frustrated members of a deprived underclass. Wealthy people pay a high price when so much of the world's resources are wasted in the perpetuation of poverty. There is the cost of security to protect rich and poor alike from those who rage against the hopelessness of poverty with violence against both property and people. And we all pay a high price for illnesses caused by the stress of dealing with the hopelessness of poverty.

People in the middle and upper classes fear that one mistake or setback, such as job loss, illness, or accident, could send them into financial depths. This fear often prevents bright people from taking risks to accomplish great things because they don't want to lose what they already have. Others counter fear by continually striving for more wealth and power, no matter how much they have. Either choice can have severe negative effects on relationships and health.

People who oppose the policies that would diminish or even bring an end to social inequities claim that ending poverty would be too expensive, but they have the numbers backward. For instance, it would cost far less to provide universal health care by directing all medical funds into medical services and bypassing greedy corporations that now grab an unhealthy chunk of that change. Ending poverty would also reduce the incidence and cost of illnesses caused by inadequate health care and its concomitant stress.

The same can be said for spending whatever it would take to provide education and job training for everyone, rather than wasting so much on fruitless social services and, especially, prisons. Indeed, there is no end to the positive comparisons that could be made between ending poverty and continuing the costly system now in place.

In fact, providing every person on the planet with all the basic goods and services necessary to enjoy a dignified existence in exchange for no more than half the amount earned by the lowest-paid full-time worker on the planet would actually cost very little. The only real social cost would be providing basic goods and services to the youngest, the oldest, and the most disabled members of society, whose payment in labor would be limited or nil.

With this plan, everyone would also have disposable income to spend on extra goods and services; everyone would be required to save a percentage of their earnings for at least five years, as detailed in the section on general tax payments in the chapter on Paying for Human Needs; and diminishing such expensive social problems as war, crime, and stress would reduce the cost of services to everyone on the planet. All those factors are among the highest goals of the capitalist philosophy; yet, oddly, many capitalists oppose policies that could eliminate poverty completely.

The only wise course, then, must be to take the simplest--and least expensive--steps necessary to end poverty and build a peaceful society around the world, for the first time in history.

COLONIALISM AND POVERTY

In the earlier section on the feudalism of labor in the chapter on Universal Employment, I discussed how the dependence of medieval serfs on their landlord foreshadowed the current labor-management dynamic. When modern workers lose their jobs, they lose all the benefits that derive from those jobs, just as ancient serfs who got thrown off the estate lost any benefits that they had received as long as they continued to serve their lord and master.

Another archaic economic policy that continues to this day is colonialism. While the modern form remains close to the traditional model, its management is less the purview of nations and now lies more in the hands of corporations. Still, countries and companies continue to cooperate for the benefit of both--at least for the benefit of leaders of the organizations involved.

Outsourcing is the backbone of modern colonialism. Millions of jobs that used to belong to workers in the most advanced countries are currently being performed by people in countries that barely developed industrially before the latter part of the 20th century, such as Mexico, India, and China. Millions more people, especially from Asia, have moved to the United States and Europe to fill technical jobs, usually for less than used to be paid to the native workers they replaced. A third group is the millions of poor people from second- and third-world countries who risk their lives to sneak into first-world nations, where they perform low-skilled jobs for low wages and no benefits.

In the United States and Europe, the most common

response to the situation is a move toward tighter immigration standards. This policy arises from a mentality that blames the most vulnerable victims in the scenario. Unfortunately, this is a response to a symptom and fails to address the cause of the problem or its effect on millions of lower- and middle-class workers.

Most people in less developed countries are unable to earn enough money to care for their families, so poverty forces them to take jobs in other locations that were formerly held by local people who are viewed as over-priced luxuries by companies that place profits above the welfare of human beings. As long as one person will perform a job for less than another person and tradition and law allow companies to operate just about any way they want, then power will remain in the hands of employers.

These policies are another way for those in power to maintain a poverty class around the world. They help corporations and governments to rein in any advancement by workers, even in first-world countries. While wealthier people benefit from low-priced goods and low-paid workers from less developed parts of the world, global job redistribution undermines most of the benefits that American workers in the middle and lower classes struggled to gain for most of the 20th century.

This situation will continue until universal standards are established for the wages and benefits given to all workers who labor in any particular job, as I proposed in the section on jobs, wages, and benefits in the chapter on Universal Employment. Colonialism in all its forms will persist until everyone is able to purchase all the basic goods and services necessary to enjoy a dignified existence in exchange for no more than half the amount earned by the lowest-paid full-time worker on the planet.

Only then will poverty become a distant memory. Only

then will everyone be able to live and work where they choose, without regard to economic conditions anywhere in the world. Only when we reach that goal everywhere on the planet will humans be able to build a peaceful society around the world, for the first time in history.

POWER, POLITICS, AND POVERTY

In previous sections in this chapter, I discussed ways in which poverty is perpetuated in our society, along with the high cost that the condition exacts from all of us, not just poor people. Yet unless we know how poverty came to exist in the first place, we'll never be able to end it. We especially need to understand why many so-called antipoverty measures accomplish so little when compared to the size of the overall problem, or even fail in the long run.

From the dawn of human history, certain people have held sway over other people and groups whom they considered to be less than they. The basis for this exercise of power began with physical strength--with stronger people claiming an advantage over those who were weaker--or mental agility--when people who mastered certain areas of knowledge considered themselves superior to those whose learning failed to match their own.

States were formed and headed by the strongest warriors who were, over time, succeeded by people who used their brains to wield power over others. The trouble is, whether they used physical or mental prowess, small groups tended to wrest control and maintain power over the majority of the people.

At first, all power and wealth was centered in the hands of the strongest, leaving most of the population to wallow in degradation. Over time, intelligent rulers allowed some of the more talented people to rise in the economic and social ranks. As this developing middle class gained a better standard of living than those who remained in a state of poverty, they tended to give credit for their good fortune to the rulers whose policies benefited them, often with little or no consideration to those who were left behind.

Gratitude for their good fortune among members of the second economic tier helped cement power for those in the highest ranks. And as I explained in the previous section on the price of poverty, people in the middle class feared plunging back into the economic depths, thus strengthening the hold that wealthy people maintained on society in general and the middle class in particular. Such is the nature of human government.

Over time, many people tried to help those who exist in a state of destitution. Some of those people could only perceive violence as an effective weapon against power. To give the devil his due, poverty and subjugation are generally the reasons--or at least the excuse--that most people give for terrorism, but one side's freedom fighter is the other side's terrorist. The sad fact is, that violent response to poverty tends to invite even stronger measures against both the terrorists and the people they fight for.

Even when violence does triumph and overcome tyranny, the new rulers tend to fall into the same power patterns they fought against in the first place, so that those who are stronger, smarter, and wealthier continue to maintain control over those with fewer resources than they enjoy. In the long run, violence is not an effective solution to the problem of poverty.

Charity does help many people in need. Uncountable

amounts of time and money are shared with people around the world in the form of food, housing, education, medical care, and other goods and services that help to ease the effects of deprivation, at least to a small degree. Still, all these good intentions are delivered in patchwork fashion, leaving many people outside the pale. Charity also tends to provide goods and services with little or no exchange of payment or labor, thus perpetuating the concept that poor people are inferior and must depend for survival on those who are stronger, smarter, and more affluent than they.

Government programs that train people to perform useful labor and help them obtain gainful employment can be beneficial, but like charity, the policies can be patchy and many have opposite effects. Welfare provides something for nothing, often accompanied by rules that prevent recipients from working and, thus, climbing out of the dark hole of poverty. A form of welfare called "workfare" allows people to perform certain types of labor, with the understanding that the jobs have little or no useful purpose. Subjects receive aid in exchange for devalued actions, solidifying the notion that these people are of little or no use to society.

In the long run, the only truly effective way to end poverty would be to create a society in which each person is able to purchase all the basic goods and services necessary for a dignified existence at a cost of no more than half the amount earned by the lowest-paid full-time worker on the planet. Thus, everyone would be able to contribute the best of their talents and skills to the vast engine that operates our global society.

Only then will poverty be relegated to a mere footnote. Only then will we be able to build a truly peaceful society around the world, for the first time in history.

INSTITUTIONS VERSUS INDIVIDUALS

As I begin writing this section, the United States is deeply engaged in the early stages of one of the most important political races of its brief history. Who will be the next president? The country--indeed, the world--needs leaders who can turn the planet back from one of the most perilous situations that humans have ever faced, in both the political and environmental arenas.

It's time to implement real solutions that won't cause more problems down the road. That'll be difficult to do, but not totally impossible. In this book, I've focused on some of the win-win-win steps we could take to end poverty everywhere and relegate war to the history books, and maybe even save the planet in the bargain.

Of course, that would require taking a new approach to the way decisions are made. In many cases, it means taking power away from the people who've led us down this road toward eventual destruction and giving it to the people it belongs to in the first place: the people who are most affected by all those decisions.

That's what democracy is all about, as opposed to a representative republic, which is the form of most governments in existence now, including the United States. That's because the republic was the best form of government that had been tried by the late 18th century, when the Founding Fathers (no mothers involved then, of course!) were organizing a new country on the American continent. Instead of trying something that was really new, they patterned their nation after the one they already knew best, with only a few minor changes.

After years of royal abuse, they put a president in charge and established the House of Representatives and the Senate. The trouble is, having one man in the top job is not far removed from handing power over to an old-fashioned monarch, and the supposedly new bicameral government merely reflected the old English Parliament with its Houses of Commons and Lords. In fact, the role of American presidents often combines the symbolism of kings (and the occasional queen) with the political power of British prime ministers. And though they claimed to have established a brand new democracy, they continued the ancient practice of limiting the right to vote to free white men of property.

It took nearly two centuries before most adults were assured the right to vote, at least on paper. Even that right is being threatened by shady shenanigans on the part of corrupt political machines. In fact, modern developments in the voting process have led to more problems for the people they were supposed to help because the old guard is just using new technology in the same old, often crooked, ways.

New institutions usually turn out to be old habits dressed up in fancy new clothes, which is why they end up being just as useless as the old ones. The reason people keep on repeating the same old mistakes after so many centuries of negative results is that few people have the courage to try any truly new ideas.

The problem is, anyone who does suggest trying something entirely new encounters strong opposition from those who choose to perpetuate the status quo, no matter how many people are hurt by it. But since all the problems that humans face were caused by doing things the same old way, it should be more than obvious that society needs to identify innovative steps that humans can take in order to turn this *Titanic* around before we reach that final, fatal "iceberg"!

And as I explained in the section on civil rights for all in the chapter on Respecting Civil Rights, the rights of every individual should be sacrosanct, so any institution that causes harm to anyone should cease these negative practices or be refused the ability to continue. Just as important, any organization that fails to serve the needs of the people it was designed to help has no reason for being.

In the current world crisis, some people who are considered to have great scientific minds claim that the solution is for humans to travel to other planets. It sounds simple, except for the megatrillion dollars and centuries of effort it would take to bring even a small part of mankind to the point where they'd be equipped to perform that operation and take the trip--if they could even identify another planet in the vast universe on which they could actually survive!

The real problem with that idea is that transporting humans who destroyed the earth in the first place into outer space so they can trash up the rest of the universe wouldn't solve anything. People have no business leaving their own back yard until they first learn to behave themselves. If we can't do the right thing here on earth, we certainly can't be expected to do so out there in the rest of the cosmos!

The only way to solve these problems is to establish entirely new ways of organizing every aspect of society. The goal of this effort should be to build a society in which each person is able to purchase all the basic goods and services necessary for a dignified existence at a cost of no more than half the amount earned by the lowest-paid full-time worker on the planet.

Only then will we be able to end poverty everywhere on the planet. Only then can we begin to build a peaceful society all around the world.

Afterword

Well, now you know how I imagine the world would be--could be--if everyone would practice real consideration and respect for each other. As I mentioned several times throughout this book, I first wrote each section of this publication as an article for the *Arizona City Independent Edition*. Since I moved to Arizona in the fall of 2000, the editor of that paper, Kayne Crison, has generously provided me with the best forum any writer could hope for: a place where I can say almost anything I want to and the freedom to experiment with new and creative ideas--a chance, one might dare to dream, to solve the problems of the world.

No matter what happens with the concepts I've expressed here, at least I've shared the principles by which I dream of a world in which everyone is treated fairly, where there is no more poverty, where no one relies on violence as a false solution to the many problems of society. I can truly say I've done my part to contribute to the conversation on how we might deal with the many perilous conditions that threaten the very survival of humanity on Planet Earth.

I close with the hope that someone somewhere will understand that we need to take safe, sane, non-toxic steps toward ending the problem of poverty around the world, so that no one will ever have any excuse to use violence to establish and maintain their influence over anyone else in the world.

Most of all, I sincerely wish for . . .

Love and peace to all,

Debbie Jordan

Index

ALSO BY Debbie Jordan

Lion's Pride

In 1911 Arizona, as Sheriff Paco Alaniz investigates the murder of Don Santiago Castillo de Leon, he must deal with the priest who seems to be more than a confessor to the distraught widow, a runaway teenager who's promised as the tenth bride to the leader of renegade Mormon polygamists, an ex-Mormon gambler who wants to save his sister and the woman he loves from the husband they both share, and a vicious mountain lion threatening inhabitants of the Territory.

Learn more at: http://lionspride